Tactics Time 2

Tactics Time 2

1001 CHESS TACTICS
from the Games of Everyday Chess Players

By Tim Brennan and Anthea Carson
http://tacticstime.com

Version 1.62

Last Updated August 5, 2014

Colofon

© 2014 New In Chess
Published by New In Chess, Alkmaar, The Netherlands
www.newinchess.com
Originally published as a Kindle edition.

Cover design: LSDDesign
Supervisor: Peter Boel
Production: Rik Weidema

Have you found any errors in this book?
Please send your remarks to editors@newinchess.com. We will collect all relevant corrections on the Errata page of our website www.newinchess.com and implement them in a possible next edition.

ISBN: 978-90-5691-537-7

Printed in Canada

Dedication

This book is dedicated to YOU, the chess player seeking improvement, wanting to win more games, and take your rating to the next level!

About the Authors

Tim Brennan is the creator of Tactics Time, which started off in 2003 as a column in the quarterly *Colorado Chess Informant* magazine. Tactics Time has grown into a blog, a free e-mail newsletter, and now a series of books! The focus has always been on real tactics from real player games, which Tim believes are the most instructive and useful types of tactics to study.

www.twitter.com/tacticstime
www.facebook.com/tacticstime
Tim@tacticstime.com

Anthea Carson is an active USCF tournament chess player, author, blogger, chess teacher, and chess mom. She is co-author of the children's chess book *How to Play Chess like an Animal* and author of various thrillers, including *The Dark Lake*.

www.twitter.com/chessanimal
www.facebook.com/AntheaJaneCarson
nth_carson@yahoo.com

Contents

Introduction

This book assumes that you already know the basics of chess (how the pieces move), terms such as 'pin', 'fork', 'skewer', and how to read algebraic notation. If you need a refresher, Wikipedia has a lot of free information on the game, en.wikipedia.org/wiki/Chess.

Puzzles are given from the point of view of the side to move. If it is Black to move, the board is shown from Black's perspective. Each solution is given on a separate page following the puzzle.

Also, be sure to **sign up** for the award winning **Tactics Time Chess Improvement e-mail newsletter**. It is free, and comes out about 3 times a week with a new chess problem for you to solve, a fun quote, chess improvement tips, and the complete game score. The main focus is on **chess improvement** and **pattern recognition**, and like this book has tons of positions that are new and never seen before from real games. You can see newsletter samples, and sign up at tacticstime.com/newsletter. You can contact us there as well if you have any questions, comments, or feedback.

Please be kind and review this book on Amazon. We need your feedback to make the next version better. You can also share this book on Facebook to your chess friends. Thank you so much!

Good luck and have fun with this book.
Happy Tactics!

Tim Brennan & Anthea Carson

1001 Chess Tactics

From the real games of everyday players

(1) Black to move

(2) Black to move

(3) White to move

(4) White to move

(5) White to move

(6) Black to move

(7) Black to move

(8) Black to move

(9) White to move

(10) Black to move

(11) Black to move

(12) Black to move

(13) Black to move

(14) White to move

(15) White to move

(16) Black to move

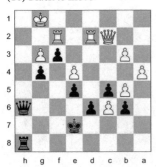

(17) Black to move

(18) Black to move

14

(19) White to move

(20) White to move

(21) White to move

(22) White to move

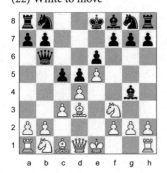

(23) White to move

(24) White to move

(25) Black to move

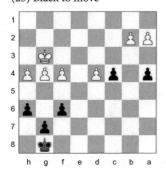

(26) White to move

(27) Black to move

(28) Black to move

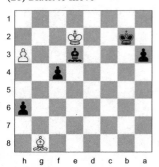

(29) White to move

(30) Black to move

(31) Black to move

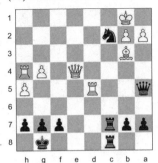

(32) Black to move

(33) White to move

(34) Black to move

(35) Black to move

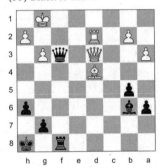

(36) White to move

(37) White to move

(38) White to move

(39) Black to move

(40) Black to move

(41) Black to move

(42) White to move

16

(43) White to move

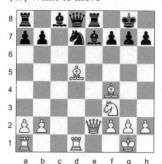

(44) White to move

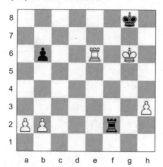

(45) Black to move

(46) White to move

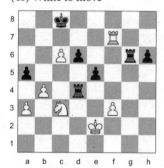

(47) White to move

(48) Black to move

(49) White to move

(50) White to move

(51) Black to move

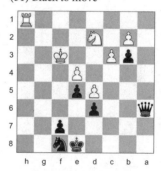

(52) White to move

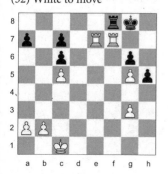

(53) Black to move

(54) White to move

17

(55) White to move

(56) Black to move

(57) Black to move

(58) Black to move

(59) Black to move

(60) White to move

(61) Black to move

(62) Black to move

(63) Black to move

(64) White to move

(65) Black to move

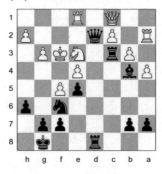

(66) Black to move

(67) Black to move

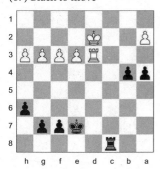

(68) White to move

(69) Black to move

(70) Black to move

(71) Black to move

(72) Black to move

(73) White to move

(74) White to move

(75) Black to move

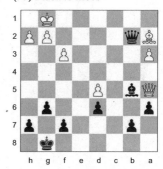

(76) Black to move

(77) White to move

(78) Black to move

19

(79) Black to move

(80) Black to move

(81) Black to move

(82) Black to move

(83) Black to move

(84) Black to move

(85) Black to move

(86) White to move

(87) White to move

(88) White to move

(89) Black to move

(90) Black to move

20

(91) White to move

(92) Black to move

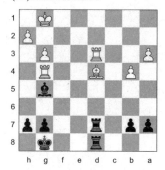

(93) Black to move

(94) White to move

(95) Black to move

(96) White to move

(97) White to move

(98) Black to move

(99) White to move

(100) Black to move

(101) White to move

(102) White to move

(103) White to move

(104) White to move

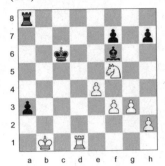

(105) Black to move

(106) Black to move

(107) White to move

(108) White to move

(109) White to move

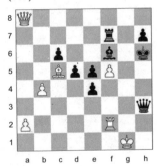

(110) Black to move

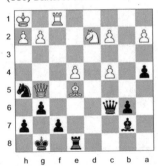

(111) White to move

(112) Black to move

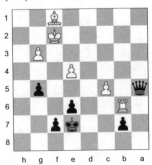

(113) Black to move

(114) White to move

22

(115) White to move

(116) Black to move

(117) White to move

(118) White to move

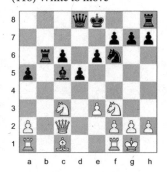

(119) White to move

(120) Black to move

(121) Black to move

(122) Black to move

(123) White to move

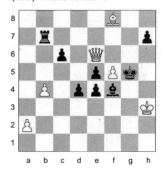

(124) White to move

(125) White to move

(126) White to move

23

(127) White to move

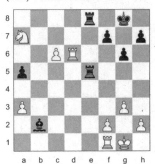

(128) White to move

(129) Black to move

(130) White to move

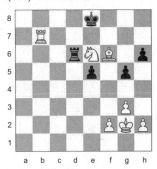

(131) White to move

(132) Black to move

(133) White to move

(134) White to move

(135) Black to move

(136) Black to move

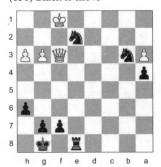

(137) Black to move

(138) White to move

24

(139) White to move

(140) Black to move

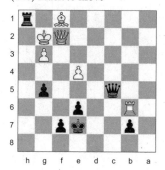

(141) Black to move

(142) White to move

(143) White to move

(144) White to move

(145) Black to move

(146) Black to move

(147) White to move

(148) Black to move

(149) White to move

(150) White to move

(151) White to move

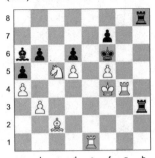

(152) White to move

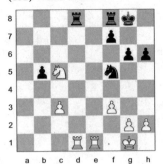

(153) Black to move

(154) Black to move

(155) Black to move

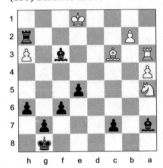

(156) White to move

(157) Black to move

(158) Black to move

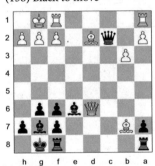

(159) White to move

(160) Black to move

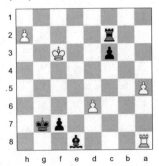

(161) White to move

(162) Black to move

26

(163) White to move

(164) Black to move

(165) Black to move

(166) Black to move

(167) Black to move

(168) Black to move

(169) Black to move

(170) White to move

(171) White to move

(172) Black to move

(173) White to move

(174) Black to move

27

(175) White to move

(176) Black to move

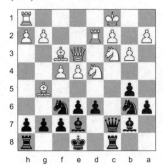

(177) White to move

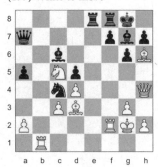

(178) White to move

(179) White to move

(180) Black to move

(181) White to move

(182) White to move

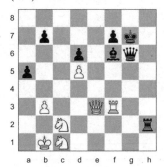

(183) Black to move

(184) Black to move

(185) Black to move

(186) Black to move

(187) Black to move

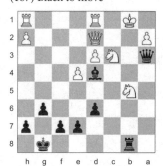

(188) White to move

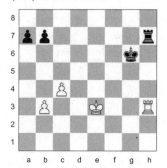

(189) Black to move

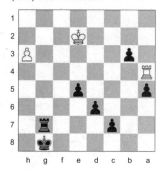

(190) Black to move

(191) White to move

(192) White to move

(193) Black to move

(194) Black to move

(195) White to move

(196) White to move

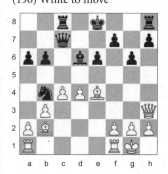

(197) White to move

(198) Black to move

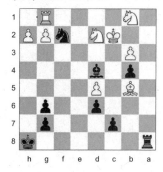

(199) Black to move

(200) White to move

(201) Black to move

(202) Black to move

(203) White to move

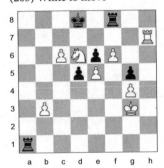

(204) White to move

(205) Black to move

(206) White to move

(207) Black to move

(208) White to move

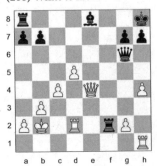

(209) White to move

(210) Black to move

(211) White to move

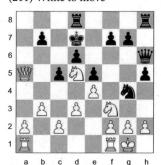

(212) White to move

(213) White to move

(214) White to move

(215) Black to move

(216) White to move

(217) White to move

(218) White to move

(219) White to move

(220) White to move

(221) White to move

(222) White to move

31

(223) White to move

(224) White to move

(225) Black to move

(226) Black to move

(227) White to move

(228) Black to move

(229) Black to move

(230) White to move

(231) Black to move

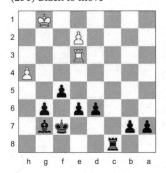

(232) White to move

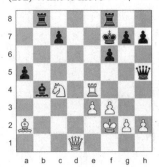

(233) White to move

(234) Black to move

32

(235) Black to move

(236) Black to move

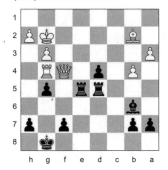

(237) Black to move

(238) Black to move

(239) White to move

(240) Black to move

(241) White to move

(242) White to move

(243) White to move

(244) Black to move

(245) White to move

(246) White to move

33

(247) White to move

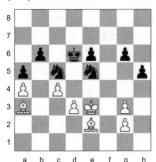

(248) White to move

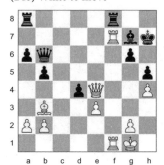

(249) White to move

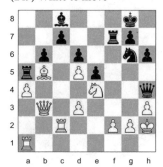

(250) Black to move

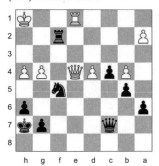

(251) White to move

(252) Black to move

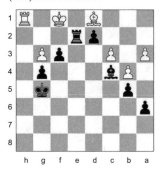

(253) Black to move

(254) White to move

(255) Black to move

(256) White to move

(257) White to move

(258) Black to move

34

(259) White to move

(260) Black to move

(261) White to move

(262) Black to move

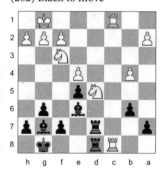

(263) Black to move

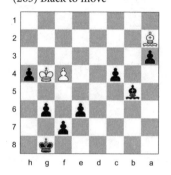

(264) Black to move

(265) Black to move

(266) White to move

(267) White to move

(268) White to move

(269) White to move

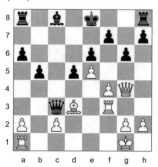

(270) Black to move

35

(271) Black to move

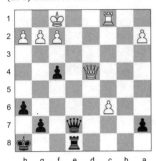

(272) White to move

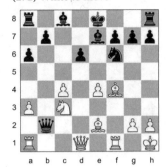

(273) White to move

(274) Black to move

(275) White to move

(276) White to move

(277) Black to move

(278) Black to move

(279) Black to move

(280) Black to move

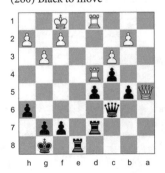

(281) Black to move

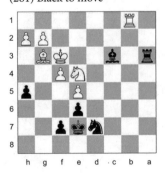

(282) Black to move

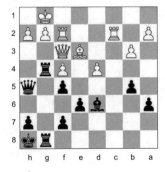

(283) White to move

(284) White to move

(285) Black to move

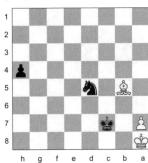

(286) White to move

(287) Black to move

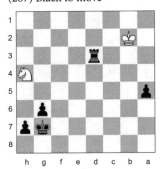

(288) Black to move

(289) Black to move

(290) White to move

(291) White to move

(292) Black to move

(293) White to move

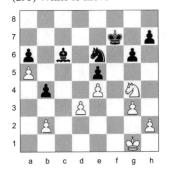

(294) Black to move

(295) White to move

(296) White to move

(297) White to move

(298) Black to move

(299) White to move

(300) Black to move

(301) Black to move

(302) White to move

(303) Black to move

(304) Black to move

(305) White to move

(306) Black to move

38

(307) White to move

(308) White to move

(309) White to move

(310) White to move

(311) Black to move

(312) Black to move

(313) Black to move

(314) White to move

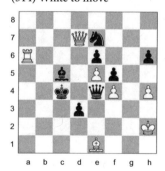

(315) White to move

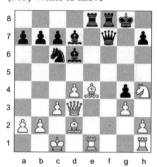

(316) Black to move

(317) White to move

(318) Black to move

(319) Black to move

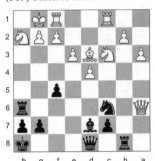

(320) White to move

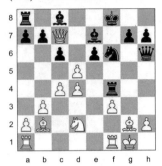

(321) Black to move

(322) White to move

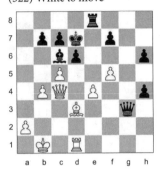

(323) Black to move

(324) Black to move

(325) White to move

(326) Black to move

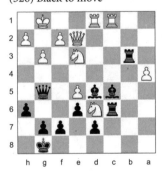

(327) Black to move

(328) Black to move

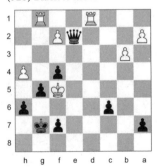

(329) White to move

(330) Black to move

(331) Black to move

(332) Black to move

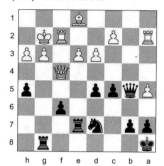

(333) White to move

(334) Black to move

(335) White to move

(336) White to move

(337) White to move

(338) Black to move

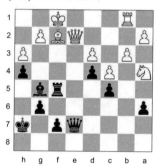

(339) Black to move

(340) Black to move

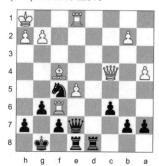

(341) Black to move

(342) Black to move

41

(343) White to move

(344) Black to move

(345) Black to move

(346) Black to move

(347) White to move

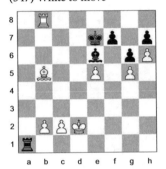

(348) Black to move

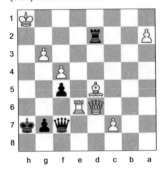

(349) White to move

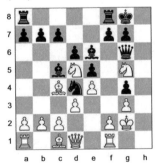

(350) White to move

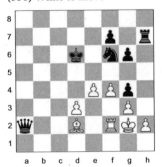

(351) Black to move

(352) White to move

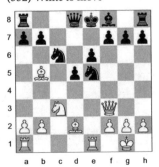

(353) Black to move

(354) Black to move

(355) Black to move

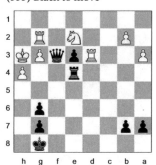

(356) White to move

(357) White to move

(358) White to move

(359) White to move

(360) White to move

(361) White to move

(362) Black to move

(363) Black to move

(364) White to move

(365) White to move

(366) Black to move

43

(367) Black to move

(368) White to move

(369) White to move

(370) White to move

(371) Black to move

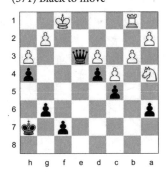

(372) White to move

(373) Black to move

(374) Black to move

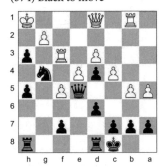

(375) Black to move

(376) White to move

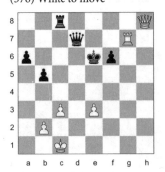

(377) White to move

(378) White to move

(379) Black to move

(380) White to move

(381) Black to move

(382) White to move

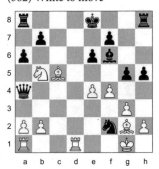

(383) White to move

(384) Black to move

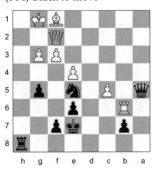

(385) Black to move

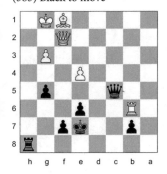

(386) Black to move

(387) White to move

(388) Black to move

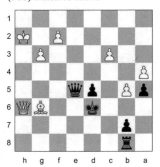

(389) White to move

(390) White to move

45

(391) White to move

(392) White to move

(393) Black to move

(394) Black to move

(395) White to move

(396) Black to move

(397) White to move

(398) White to move

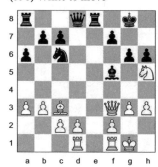

(399) White to move

(400) White to move

(401) White to move

(402) Black to move

(403) White to move

(404) Black to move

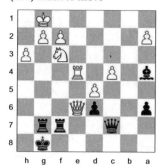

(405) White to move

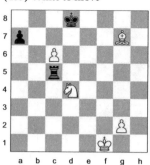

(406) Black to move

(407) White to move

(408) Black to move

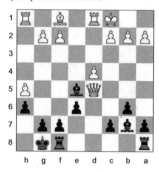

(409) White to move

(410) White to move

(411) White to move

(412) White to move

(413) White to move

(414) White to move

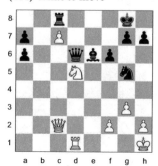

47

(415) Black to move

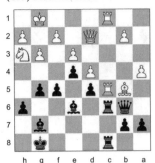

(416) White to move

(417) White to move

(418) White to move

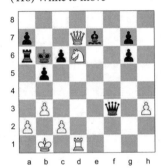

(419) White to move

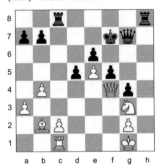

(420) White to move

(421) White to move

(422) Black to move

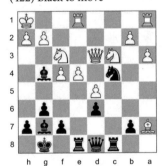

(423) Black to move

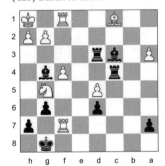

(424) White to move

(425) Black to move

(426) White to move

48

(427) White to move

(428) Black to move

(429) White to move

(430) White to move

(431) White to move

(432) White to move

(433) White to move

(434) Black to move

(435) White to move

(436) White to move

(437) White to move

(438) White to move

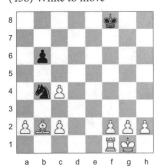

49

(439) White to move

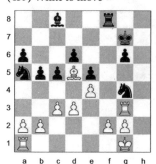

(440) White to move

(441) White to move

(442) White to move

(443) White to move

(444) White to move

(445) Black to move

(446) Black to move

(447) Black to move

(448) Black to move

(449) White to move

(450) White to move

50

(451) Black to move

(452) Black to move

(453) White to move

(454) Black to move

(455) White to move

(456) Black to move

(457) Black to move

(458) Black to move

(459) White to move

(460) Black to move

(461) Black to move

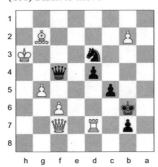

(462) White to move

51

(463) Black to move

(464) Black to move

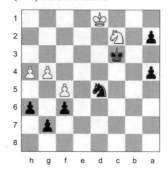

(465) Black to move

(466) Black to move

(467) Black to move

(468) White to move

(469) White to move

(470) White to move

(471) Black to move

(472) White to move

(473) Black to move

(474) Black to move

52

(475) White to move

(476) White to move

(477) White to move

(478) White to move

(479) Black to move

(480) White to move

(481) White to move

(482) White to move

(483) White to move

(484) White to move

(485) Black to move

(486) Black to move

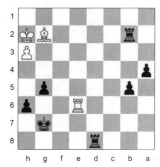

(487) Black to move

(488) White to move

(489) White to move

(490) White to move

(491) Black to move

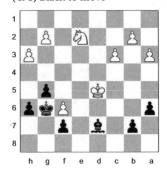

(492) White to move

(493) White to move

(494) Black to move

(495) White to move

(496) White to move

(497) Black to move

(498) Black to move

(499) White to move

(500) Black to move

(501) Black to move

(502) Black to move

(503) Black to move

(504) White to move

(505) White to move

(506) White to move

(507) White to move

(508) White to move

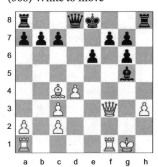

(509) Black to move

(510) Black to move

55

(511) Black to move

(512) White to move

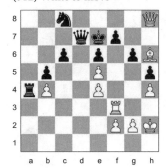

(513) White to move

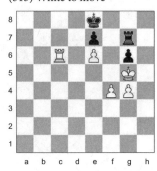

(514) White to move

(515) White to move

(516) White to move

(517) White to move

(518) White to move

(519) Black to move

(520) White to move

(521) Black to move

(522) Black to move

(523) Black to move

(524) White to move

(525) Black to move

(526) Black to move

(527) White to move

(528) White to move

(529) White to move

(530) White to move

(531) Black to move

(532) Black to move

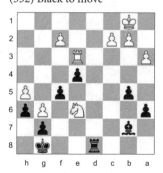

(533) Black to move

(534) White to move

57

(535) White to move

(536) Black to move

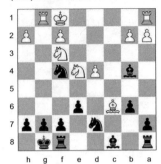

(537) Black to move

(538) Black to move

(539) Black to move

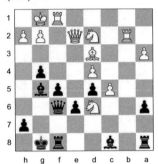

(540) Black to move

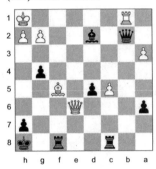

(541) Black to move

(542) Black to move

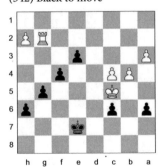

(543) Black to move

(544) Black to move

(545) White to move

(546) White to move

58

(547) White to move

(548) Black to move

(549) Black to move

(550) Black to move

(551) Black to move

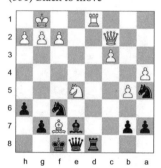

(552) Black to move

(553) Black to move

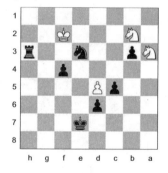

(554) Black to move

(555) White to move

(556) White to move

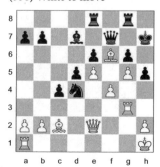

(557) White to move

(558) White to move

59

(559) White to move

(560) Black to move

(561) Black to move

(562) Black to move

(563) White to move

(564) White to move

(565) Black to move

(566) White to move

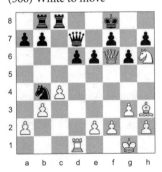

(567) White to move

(568) Black to move

(569) White to move

(570) White to move

60

(571) Black to move

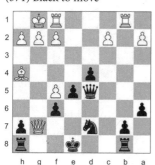

(572) White to move

(573) Black to move

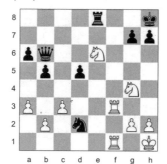

(574) Black to move

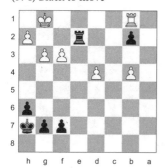

(575) White to move

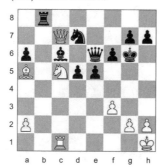

(576) White to move

(577) White to move

(578) Black to move

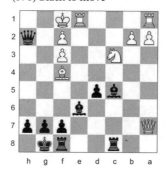

(579) White to move

(580) White to move

(581) White to move

(582) White to move

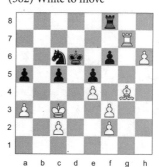

(583) White to move

(584) White to move

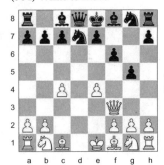

(585) White to move

(586) White to move

(587) Black to move

(588) Black to move

(589) Black to move

(590) Black to move

(591) White to move

(592) Black to move

(593) Black to move

(594) Black to move

62

(595) White to move

(596) White to move

(597) White to move

(598) Black to move

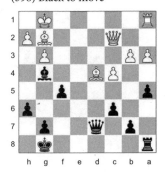

(599) White to move

(600) White to move

(601) Black to move

(602) Black to move

(603) White to move

(604) Black to move

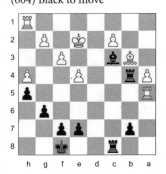

(605) Black to move

(606) White to move

(607) White to move

(608) Black to move

(609) White to move

(610) White to move

(611) Black to move

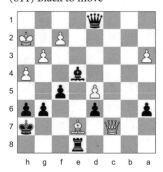

(612) White to move

(613) White to move

(614) Black to move

(615) White to move

(616) Black to move

(617) White to move

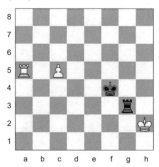

(618) White to move

(619) Black to move

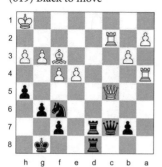

(620) Black to move

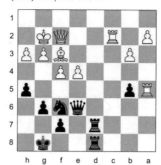

(621) White to move

(622) Black to move

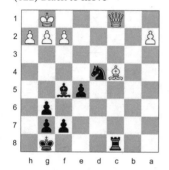

(623) Black to move

(624) Black to move

(625) White to move

(626) White to move

(627) Black to move

(628) White to move

(629) White to move

(630) White to move

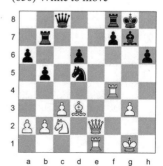

65

(631) White to move

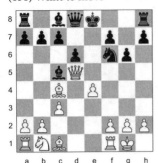

(632) Black to move

(633) Black to move

(634) Black to move

(635) Black to move

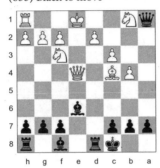

(636) Black to move

(637) White to move

(638) Black to move

(639) White to move

(640) White to move

(641) Black to move

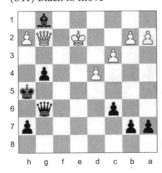

(642) Black to move

66

(643) White to move

(644) White to move

(645) Black to move

(646) White to move

(647) Black to move

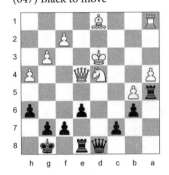

(648) Black to move

(649) Black to move

(650) Black to move

(651) White to move

(652) White to move

(653) White to move

(654) Black to move

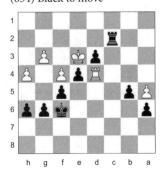

67

(655) Black to move

(656) White to move

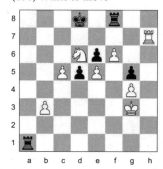

(657) White to move

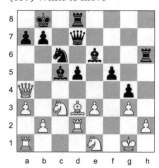

(658) White to move

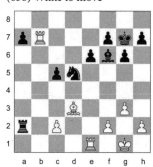

(659) Black to move

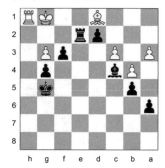

(660) White to move

(661) Black to move

(662) Black to move

(663) White to move

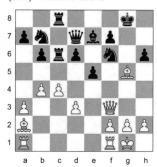

(664) White to move

(665) White to move

(666) White to move

(667) White to move

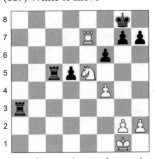

(668) Black to move

(669) White to move

(670) White to move

(671) Black to move

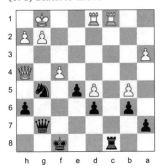

(672) White to move

(673) Black to move

(674) White to move

(675) Black to move

(676) White to move

(677) White to move

(678) White to move

69

(679) White to move

(680) Black to move

(681) White to move

(682) Black to move

(683) Black to move

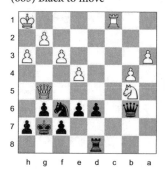

(684) White to move

(685) White to move

(686) White to move

(687) White to move

(688) White to move

(689) Black to move

(690) Black to move

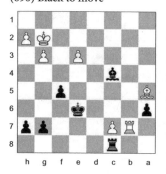

(691) White to move

(692) White to move

(693) Black to move

(694) Black to move

(695) Black to move

(696) Black to move

(697) White to move

(698) Black to move

(699) White to move

(700) White to move

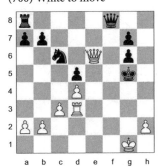

(701) Black to move

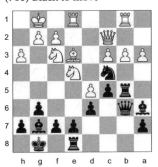

(702) White to move

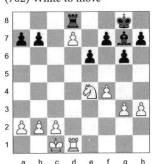

71

(703) White to move

(704) Black to move

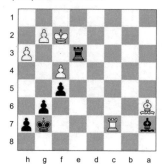

(705) White to move

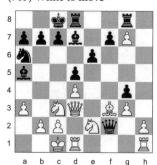

(706) White to move

(707) White to move

(708) White to move

(709) Black to move

(710) Black to move

(711) Black to move

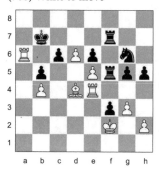

(712) White to move

(713) White to move

(714) White to move

72

(715) Black to move

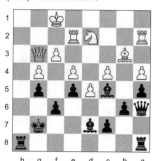

(716) White to move

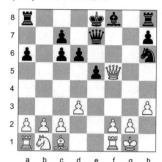

(717) White to move

(718) White to move

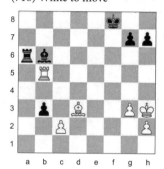

(719) Black to move

(720) Black to move

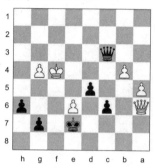

(721) White to move

(722) Black to move

(723) White to move

(724) Black to move

(725) White to move

(726) White to move

73

(727) Black to move

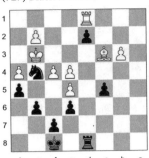

(728) White to move

(729) White to move

(730) White to move

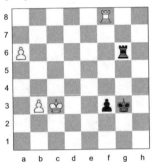

(731) White to move

(732) White to move

(733) Black to move

(734) White to move

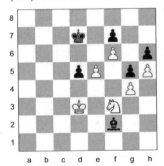

(735) Black to move

(736) White to move

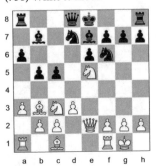

(737) Black to move

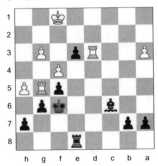

(738) Black to move

74

(739) Black to move

(740) Black to move

(741) Black to move

(742) White to move

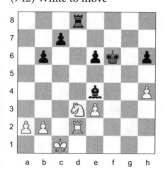

(743) White to move

(744) White to move

(745) White to move

(746) White to move

(747) Black to move

(748) Black to move

(749) Black to move

(750) White to move

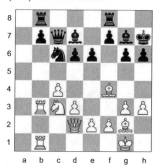

75

(751) White to move

(752) Black to move

(753) White to move

(754) Black to move

(755) Black to move

(756) Black to move

(757) Black to move

(758) Black to move

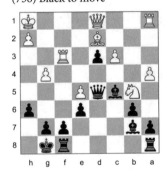

(759) Black to move

(760) Black to move

(761) Black to move

(762) Black to move

(763) Black to move

(764) Black to move

(765) Black to move

(766) Black to move

(767) Black to move

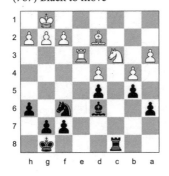

(768) Black to move

(769) Black to move

(770) White to move

(771) Black to move

(772) Black to move

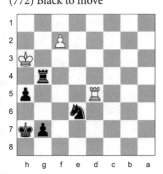

(773) Black to move

(774) Black to move

77

(775) Black to move

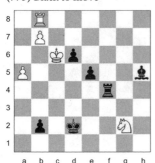

(776) White to move

(777) White to move

(778) White to move

(779) Black to move

(780) Black to move

(781) White to move

(782) White to move

(783) White to move

(784) Black to move

(785) Black to move

(786) White to move

78

(787) White to move

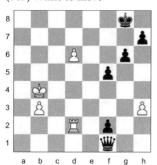

(788) White to move

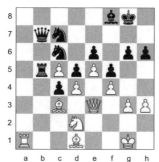

(789) White to move

(790) White to move

(791) White to move

(792) White to move

(793) White to move

(794) Black to move

(795) White to move

(796) Black to move

(797) White to move

(798) White to move

79

(799) White to move

(800) Black to move

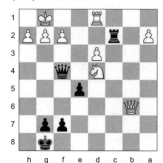

(801) Black to move

(802) Black to move

(803) Black to move

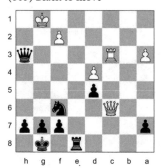

(804) Black to move

(805) Black to move

(806) Black to move

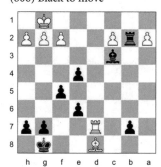

(807) Black to move

(808) White to move

(809) Black to move

(810) White to move

(811) White to move

(812) Black to move

(813) Black to move

(814) Black to move

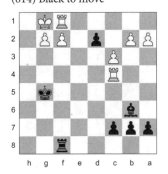

(815) White to move

(816) White to move

(817) Black to move

(818) White to move

(819) White to move

(820) Black to move

(821) Black to move

(822) White to move

(823) White to move

(824) Black to move

(825) Black to move

(826) Black to move

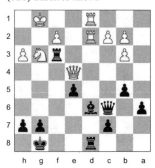

(827) White to move

(828) Black to move

(829) White to move

(830) White to move

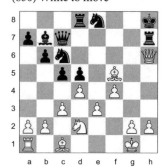

(831) Black to move

(832) White to move

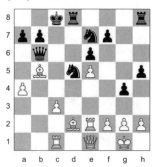

(833) Black to move

(834) White to move

(835) White to move

(836) Black to move

(837) White to move

(838) White to move

(839) White to move

(840) White to move

(841) White to move

(842) White to move

(843) Black to move

(844) White to move

(845) White to move

(846) White to move

83

(847) White to move

(848) Black to move

(849) White to move

(850) White to move

(851) Black to move

(852) White to move

(853) White to move

(854) Black to move

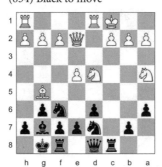

(855) White to move

(856) White to move

(857) Black to move

(858) Black to move

(859) White to move

(860) White to move

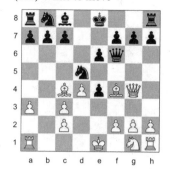

(861) White to move

(862) White to move

(863) Black to move

(864) Black to move

(865) Black to move

(866) Black to move

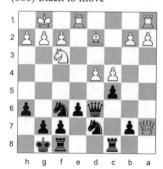

(867) Black to move

(868) Black to move

(869) White to move

(870) White to move

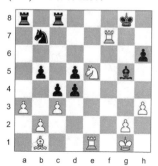

85

(871) White to move

(872) Black to move

(873) White to move

(874) White to move

(875) White to move

(876) White to move

(877) White to move

(878) White to move

(879) White to move

(880) White to move

(881) Black to move

(882) White to move

(883) Black to move

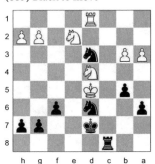

(884) Black to move

(885) White to move

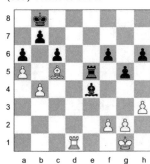

(886) White to move

(887) Black to move

(888) White to move

(889) White to move

(890) White to move

(891) White to move

(892) Black to move

(893) Black to move

(894) Black to move

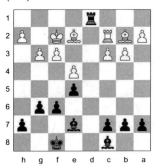

(895) White to move

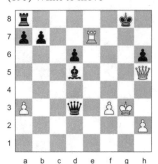

(896) Black to move

(897) Black to move

(898) Black to move

(899) Black to move

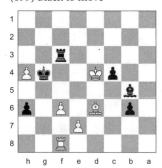

(900) White to move

(901) White to move

(902) White to move

(903) Black to move

(904) Black to move

(905) Black to move

(906) Black to move

88

(907) Black to move

(908) Black to move

(909) Black to move

(910) Black to move

(911) Black to move

(912) White to move

(913) White to move

(914) Black to move

(915) White to move

(916) Black to move

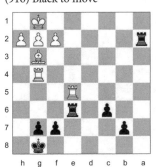

(917) White to move

(918) White to move

(919) White to move

(920) White to move

(921) White to move

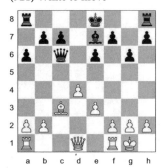

(922) White to move

(923) White to move

(924) Black to move

(925) Black to move

(926) Black to move

(927) White to move

(928) White to move

(929) Black to move

(930) White to move

90

(931) White to move

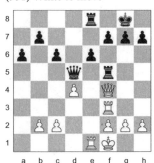

(932) White to move

(933) White to move

(934) White to move

(935) White to move

(936) White to move

(937) White to move

(938) White to move

(939) Black to move

(940) Black to move

(941) White to move

(942) White to move

(943) Black to move

(944) Black to move

(945) Black to move

(946) White to move

(947) White to move

(948) Black to move

(949) White to move

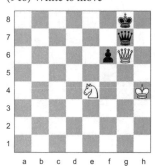

(950) Black to move

(951) White to move

(952) Black to move

(953) White to move

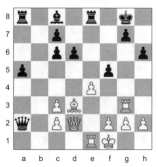

(954) Black to move

92

(955) White to move

(956) White to move

(957) White to move

(958) White to move

(959) Black to move

(960) Black to move

(961) Black to move

(962) Black to move

(963) Black to move

(964) Black to move

(965) White to move

(966) Black to move

(967) Black to move

(968) White to move

(969) Black to move

(970) Black to move

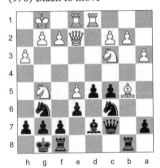

(971) White to move

(972) Black to move

(973) Black to move

(974) White to move

(975) Black to move

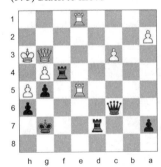

(976) Black to move

(977) White to move

(978) White to move

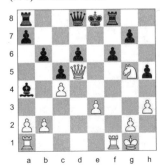

94

(979) White to move

(980) Black to move

(981) Black to move

(982) Black to move

(983) Black to move

(984) White to move

(985) White to move

(986) White to move

(987) Black to move

(988) Black to move

(989) White to move

(990) Black to move

95

(991) White to move

(992) Black to move

(993) Black to move

(994) Black to move

(995) Black to move

(996) Black to move

(997) White to move

(998) White to move

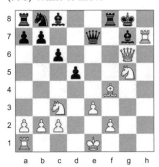

(999) White to move

(1000) White to move

(1001) White to move

Solutions

(1)

In this position, the white queen on h5 cannot be captured by the g-pawn because of the pin on the g file by the white rook on g1. The white queen is also attacking Black's knight on h6.

Black solves this problem with *26...Qxg1+!!*. After either *27.Kxg1* or *27.Nxg1*, Black can safely play *27...gxh5*, winning a rook.

(2)

9...Qe4+ forks the white king and white bishop on f4 *10.Kf2 Qxf4*.

(3)

15.Bxe6+! double attack: g4/g8. *15...dxe6 16.Qxe6+ Kh8 17.Nf7+* discovered attack on the black queen. *17...Rxf7 18.Bxc7* (*17...Kg8* leads to a smothered mate, *18.Nh6+ Kh8 19.Qg8+ Rxg8 20.Nf7#*.)

(4)

18.Ng6 forks the black queen and rook, taking advantage of the pinned f-pawn.

(5)

13.Qh6 and Black cannot stop *14.Qh8#*.

(6)

10...Qh4+ forks the white king and bishop.

(7)

12...Qh4 and Black cannot defend the h2-pawn. *13.h3 Qxg3 14.hxg4 Bxg4* wins the pawn.

(8)

5...Bb4 pins the white queen to the king.

(9)

24.Nd7 forks the two black rooks.

(10)

15...Rd1+!! sets up a deadly double discovered check, *16.Kxd1 Ba4+ 17.Ke1 Qd1#*.

(11)

17...Rb1+!! 18.Nxb1 Bb2#.

(12)

36...Nd3 attacks the white rook on e1 and threatens the mate *37...Rc5#*. White cannot meet both threats without giving up material.

(13)

10...Bxf3 11.gxf3 is the only way to recapture. *11...Qb4+* forks the white king and bishop, winning a piece. Note that taking the knight first prevented the move Nd2, blocking the check, and defending the bishop on c4.

(14)

40.Bg8+!! creates a discovered attack on the queen on a3, *40...Rxg8 41.Qxa3*.

(15)
20.exd7#.

(16)
47...Qh1#.

(17)

16...Qe3+ checks the white king and adds a second attacker to the bishop on c3. *17.Kh1 Bxc3* wins a piece.

(18)

32...Nf4+ forks the white king and bishop on d5, and will win the white queen on the next move.

(19)

10.Nxf7! sets up a double attack on a8 and f7, so *10...Kxf7 11.Qf3+ Kg8 12.Qxa8* picks up the loose rook on a8.

(20)
21.Qxg6+!! hxg6 22.Rh8+ Kf7 23.Ng5#.

(21)
18.Qxg6#.

(22)
7.Qa4+ Nd7 8.dxc5 creates a discovered attack. *8… Qxc5 9.Qxg4* wins a piece.

(23)
16.Ne4 forks the black queen and bishop. There is no square where the black queen can retreat and still protect the bishop, so White wins a piece, *16… Qd7 17.Nxc5*.

(24)
19.Qg4+ Kh8 20.Qg7#.

(25)
45…a3! forces the win. *46.bxa3 47.c3* or *46.b3 cxb3 47.axb3 a2* and Black will promote.

(26)
11.f5 traps the black bishop on e6, which has no escape squares.

(27)
41…Rc4+ 42.Ka3 Ra4#.

(28)
46…a2 forces White to give up his bishop. *47.Bxa2 Kxa2* allows Black to transpose into a winning endgame.

(29)
22.f6 forks the black knight and bishop.

(30)
12…a6 starts a wave of deadly pawn pushes. *13.Na3* leaves only one safe square for the knight. *13…b5* attacks the bishop and threatens *14…b4*, forking the white knights on a3 and c3. White's best option is to give up a piece for two pawns, *14.Naxb5 axb5 15.Bxb5*.

(31)
29…Na3+!. 30.bxa3 Rc1+ 31.Kb2 Qc3#,
or
30.Ka1 Rc1+ 31.Qb1 Rxb1#.

(32)
25…Bxd4 26.Nxd4 Rxd4! takes advantage of the pinned c-pawn, winning a piece.

(33)
36.Nf7#.

(34)
17…Rfb8 traps the white queen *18.Bf4 Qxf4 19.Qa6* and Black is up a piece.

(35)
36…Bxd4+ overloads the white defense. *37.Rf2 [37.Qxd4 Qf1#] Qxf2+ 38.Kh1 Qg1#.*

(36)
14.Qxg7 takes a pawn, and attacks the undefended rook on h8. In the game, White played 14.Qc3 to defend the d4-pawn, which is much more passive.

(37)
14.Nf5 forks the black queen and d6-pawn, which cannot be defended, *14…Qd8 15.Nxd6.*

(38)
24.Nd6+ and a double discovered check leads to mate *24…Kd8 [24…Kf8 25.Qf7#] 25.Qe8+ Rxe8 26.Nf7#*, with a smothered mate in the middle of the board.

(39)
22…Rxc7 takes a piece that is attacked twice and only defended once.

(40)
18…Qf2+ 19.Kh1 Qxh2# is a common mating pattern between queen and knight.

(41)
14…Qxc3+ takes a pawn, and forks the white king and rook.

(42)
17.Rd7 forks the two black bishops.

(43)
14.Bxf7+. 14…Kxf7 15.Qc4+ (15. Ne5+ is good also) *Kf8 16.Bc7* traps the black queen. If the black king moves out of check, White can win the exchange with *15.Bxe8.*

(44)
43.Re8+ forces a trade to an easily won endgame, *43…Rf8 44.Rxf8+ Kxf8.*

(45)
24…Rd1+ leads to a back-rank mate, *25.Rf1 Rxf1#.*

(46)
34.Nb5 attacks the black rook on d4 and threatens the mate **35. Rf8#**. Black cannot meet both threats. The game continued **34...Rc4 35.Rf8#**.

(47)
21.Bxg7+ creates a discovered attack, **21...Kxg7 22.Qxd6**.

(48)
17...Nxc3 removes the defender of the knight on e5, **18.bxc3 Bxe5**.

(49)
16.Bf1 traps the black queen.

(50)
8.Bb5!! decoy for **8...Qxb5 9.Nxc7+** with a family fork.

(51)
34...Qd3+ forks the white king and knight.

(52)
35.Rg7+ Kh8 36.Rh7+ Kg8 37.Reg7# is a common mating pattern with two rooks on the seventh rank.

(53)
38...Rg8+ overloads the white king, **39.Kf3 Kxf5**.

(54)
35.Ng6+ forks the black king and queen.

(55)
32.Qxg4!! wins a piece that appears to be defended, if **32...Qxg4 33.Nh6#**.

(56)
20...Rxh3#, the g2-pawn is pinned by the bishop on b7.

(57)
32...Re1+! deflection onto **33.Qxe1 Qxf3+ 34.Kg1 h2# (34...Qg2#)**.

(58)
14...Qxg1+!. Both queens are under attack, so Black sacrifices his with check before capturing White's queen. In-between moves like this are easy to miss. **15.Rxg1 fxe2** and Black is up a piece.

(59)
9...Bxg3+! wins a pawn. If **10.hxg3 Qxh1**, Black picks up the exchange as well.

(60)
13.Bb5+ wins the queen with a discovered check, **13...c6 14.Qxh1**.

(61)
24...Rxd6 wins a piece back. White cannot recapture because **25.Nxd6 Nf2+** forks the white king and queen.

(62)
32...Rh2 traps the white queen.

(63)
22...Qxg3! wins a piece (the f2-pawn is pinned) and threatens mate on h2. If **23.hxg4 Nf3+ 24.Kh1 Qh2#**

(64)
26.Nxe5+ discovered check **26...Rxd5 27.Nxg6**.

(65)
25...Rxe3+!. Deflection: **26.Rxe3 Qxc1**.

(66)
6...Qa5+ forks the king and the bishop on f5, **7.Nc3 Qxf5**.

(67)
37...b3 and Black has reached her goal, **38.axb3 a3**.

(68)
25.Nxe5, and the pawn on d6 can't recapture because it's pinned.

(69)
27...Nxg3+ 28.Kh2 Qh4+ 29.Kg1 Nxe2#.

(70)
35...Rh3+ 36.gxh3 Qxh3#,
or **35...Qh3+ 36.gxh3 Rxh3#**.

(71)
21...Nh2! clears the f3-square, attacking the queen and threatening **22...Bf3+**, forking the white king and queen. White has no good squares to move the queen. For example, **22.Qg5** or **22.Qh4 Rxf2+** creates a discovered attack on the queen, or **22.Qh5 Bf3+** forks the white king and queen.

(72)
16...Nxf4 17.Qxf4 f6 attacks the pinned knight.
18.Qe3 fxe5 wins a piece.

(73)
19.Rh1 traps the black queen.

(74)
24.Qxf5 takes the rook and the bishop is pinned.

(75)
23...Qd4+ 24.Kh1 Qd1+ 25.Qe1 Qxe1#.

(76)
12...e3 blocks the white queen's defense of the knight on g5.

(77)
15.Nxf6+ removes the defender of the h7-pawn,
15...exf6 16.Qxh7+.

(78)
25...e3 attacks the white queen, and cuts off the defense of the white rook. **26.Qxd3 Qxh6** wins the exchange, or
26.Rxg6 exd2+ 27.Kxd2 fxg6 28.Kxd3 also wins the exchange.

(79)
33...Qe2#.

(80)
17...Rab8 and the white queen cannot move because of the back-rank mate threat of Rb1#.
18.Qxb8 Rxb8.

(81)
9...c5, the Noah's Ark Trap. **10.Qd1 c4** traps the white bishop.

(82)
43...f3+ creates a discovered check, **44.Kh3 Rh1#.**

(83)
17...Qf2+ 18.Kxe4 f5+ 19.Kd3 Rfd8 pins the white queen to the king.

(84)
19...Rxf7 takes a piece that is attacked twice and only defended once. The queen on h2 protects the black rook on b8.

(85)
13...Bb4 pins the white queen to the king, if **14.c3 dxc3 15.bxc3 Bxc3**

(86)
24.Bf4 Rh5 25.g4 forks the black rook and bishop, or **24...Rh4 25.Bg5** forks the black queen and rook.

(87)
17.Qf6 and mate on g7 cannot be stopped, **17... Qd1+ 18.Rxd1 Nc5 19.Qg7#.**

(88)
34.Rd7! adds a second attacker to the pinned black rook on g7. Black has no easy way to defend this rook. Giving up the queen leads to mate **34... Qg8 35.Bxg8 Ne7 36.Rxe7 Kxg8 37.Qxg7#**. Black cannot capture the rook because of **34...Qxd7 35.Qf8+ Rg8 36.Qxg8#.**

(89)
47...Rf6+ deflects the king from the defense of the rook, **48.Kg1 Rxe2**. If **48.Rf2 Re1+ 49.Rxe1 dxe1=Q#**

(90)
24...Qxg2#.

(91)
49.Bh5+ overloads the black king **49...Kxh5 50.Qxf6.**

(92)
30...Rxd4! wins a piece. **31.Rdxd4 Be3+** double attack, or **31.Rgxd4 Rxd4 32.Rxd4 Be3+.**

(93)
34...Rc3 forks the white queen, and adds a second attacker to the white knight on g3. White will lose a piece.

(94)
21.Ng3 traps the black queen. **21...Qh4 22.Nf5+** forks the black king and queen.

(95)
29...Qe1+ forks the white king and rook on a5.
30.Kg2 Qxa5 wins a piece.

(96)
21.Qc3+ forks the black king and knight on c7, attacking a second time.

(97)
20.Rxf7+!! takes a pawn that only appears to be defended. **20...Bxf7 21.Qxh7#**, or **20...Rxf7 21.Ne6+** forks the black king and queen, and leads to mate **21.Kh8 22.Qxd8+ Rf8 23.Qxf8#**.

(98)
39...Qxc4 40.Rxc4 Rd1+ 41.Kg2 Rd2 pins and wins the bishop.

(99)
9.Nxd4 and if Black recaptures, **9...Qxd4 10.Bb5+!!** wins the queen.

(100)
48...Qxe3!! 49.Qxe3 d2, and the pawn cannot be stopped.

(101)
31.Rxf6 wins a piece. The g-pawn is pinned, preventing **32.Qg8#**.

(102)
11.Bxg5 overloads the black queen. **11...Qxg5 12.Nc7+** forks the black king and rook.

(103)
13.Qh5#. Black played **12...g5??** on the previous move to attack the white bishop on h4, but missed this "Fool's Mate" pattern.

(104)
32.Rd6+ forks the black king and bishop.

(105)
23...Qg5+ 24.Kh2 Qg2#.

(106)
16...Qf3 and while White has some spite checks, mate with **...Qg2#** cannot be stopped.

(107)
27.Qh8+ Ke7 28.Qe8#.

(108)
28.Qe8+ Qxe8 29.Rxe8+ Kf7 30.R1e7#.

(109)
44.Rh2 pins the black queen to the king.

(110)
25...h6 deflects the white queen from defense of the white bishop, **26.Qxh6 Rxe5**.

(111)
14.Nb6+ forks the black king and queen.

(112)
41...Qxc5+ forks the white king and rook.

(113)
21...Rc1+ creates a discovered attack on the white queen, **22.Rxc1 Qxd4**.

(114)
19.Ng7+ Ke7 20.Bg5#.

(115)
24.Qc3 attacks the black knight, which is pinned to the rook on h8, and cannot be defended. **24...Bf6 25.Nxf6** removes the defender.

(116)
13...Bxg3 threatens mate and White cannot capture the bishop because of **14.fxg3 Qxg3#**. White's best defense still leads to mate, **14.d4 e3 15.Qd2 Qxf2+ 16.Kd1 Qxf1+ 17.Qe1 Qxe1#**.

(117)
15.Bg5 adds a second attacker to the black knight with an uncomfortable pin. The knight cannot be adequately defended. For example, **15...Kg7 16.Bxf6+ Qxf6 17.Rxf6 Kxf6** leaves White ahead a rook for a queen.

(118)
15.Na4 Bd6 16.Nxb6 wins the exchange.

(119)
22.Rxe3 gets the rook out of danger and captures the unprotected knight.

(120)
29...e4+ checks the White king with a discovered attack on the rook on c4 **30. Kxe4 Rxc4**.

(121)
12...Nxd4 wins a piece. **13.Qxd4?? Bxh2+** creates a discovered attack on the queen, **14.Kxh2 Qxd4**.

(122)
9...Nxe4 wins a pawn. **10.Bxe4 Qxh4+** forks the white king and bishop.

(123)
51.Bh6+ Kh5 52.Qf6 Bxh6 53.Qh4# is a cute way to finish the game.

(124)
27.Bxf6 Kg8 28.Be6+ Kh8 29.Qxh6#, or *27...Bxf6 28.Qxh6+ Qh7 29.Qxh7#*.

(125)
32.hxg7+ creates a double discovered check *32...Kg8 33.Rh8#*. White is up 2 pieces, but missed multiple kill shots in this game. In this position White got too cute with *32.Rxg7??*, hoping for a windmill style discovered check, and missed that his opponent can play *32...Qxc2#*, which is what happened.

(126)
18.f4 attacks the pinned black bishop *18...0-0 19.fxe5*.

(127)
26.c7 and Black will have to give up a rook after White queens his pawn. For example, *26...Rc5 27.Rd8 Rf8 28.Rxf8 Kxf8 29.c8=Q+ Rxc8 30.Nxc8*.

(128)
8.Nxd4 wins a piece, *8...Bxe2 9.Nxe2* or *8...Qxd4 9.Bxg4*.

(129)
25...Nxf3+, and the g2-pawn is pinned, *26.Kh1 Ng3#*.

(130)
47.Re7#.

(131)
27.Rxd2, and the e3-pawn is pinned to the queen. The white knight on c3 covers the d1-square.

(132)
14...Ne5 attacks the white queen and adds a second attacker to the white bishop on c4. White loses a piece.

(133)
29.Qxc6!! and Black cannot recapture because of the checkmate *29...Bxc6 30.Rd8+ Be8 31.Rxe8#*.

(134)
26.Qxf7+ takes a pawn and forks the black king and knight, *26...Kh8 27.Qxb3*.

(135)
31...Bxf1 takes a piece that is attacked twice and only defended once.

(136)
36...Nd2+ forks the White king and queen.

(137)
22...Rxc3 captures the white bishop, defended through an X-ray from the black queen.

(138)
24.Qg5#.

(139)
12.Nf7 forks the black rooks.

(140)
41...Rh2+ skewers the white king and queen, *42.Kxh2 Qxf2+*.

(141)
46...Ne3 attacks the rook and threatens *47...Qg2#*. White cannot meet both threats.

(142)
15.Qf3 forks the bishop on f5 and the rook on a8.

(143)
18.Qf7#.

(144)
13.Qc4 d5 14.Qxd5 cxb2 15.Qf7#.

(145)
34...Qh5#.

(146)
28...Qxe4 wins the rook. White cannot recapture because of *29.Rxe4?? Rd1+ 30.Re1 Rxe1#*

(147)
33.Qxe3+ wins a pawn, and forces a trade of queens, transposing into an easily won endgame.

(148)
20...h5 attacks the pinned white bishop.

(149)
14.Bg5+ skewers the black king and queen. *14... Kg7* or *14...Ke6 15.Bxd8*.

(150)
17.Nd5 forks the black queen and bishop.

(151)
40.Nd7#.

(152)
32.Nd7 wins the exchange. If 32...Re8 33.Nf6+ forks the black king and rook.

(153)
33...Rg3 is a clever way to add a second attacker to the g2-pawn, because of the pin on the f2-pawn by the black bishop, **34.Ne3 Bxe3 35.fxe3 Rxg2+**.

(154)
34...Bxg2+ overloads the white king, **35.Kxg2 Rxe1** or **35.Ke2 Bf3+ 36.Kxf3 Rxe1**. Both variations win a rook and pawn for a bishop.

(155)
42...Be3 creates a mating net. White cannot stop **43...Rh1#**.

(156)
23.Ng6#.

(157)
38...Be7+ 39.Kh6 Rh4#.

(158)
17...Rad8 skewers the white queen and bishop.

(159)
32.Rd8 and Black will have to give up all their material to avoid the mating net. White's threat is **32...Rxd8 33.Rxd8+** and Black has to give up the queen with **33...Qxd8** or else **33...Kh7 34.Rh8#**.

(160)
47...Bc6+ forks the white king and rook.

(161)
28.Qxa8!! wins the black rook. Black cannot recapture because of **28...Rxa8 29.Nf7#**.

(162)
27...Rf4 gets the black rook out of danger, and adds a second attacker to the white knight, which cannot be defended twice. The white knight is preventing the move Rg1+ skewering the white king and rook on a1. White will lose material.

(163)
19.b4 forks the black queen and knight.

(164)
15...h3 leads to mate for Black. **16.g3 Qf3**, and mate with **...Qg2#** cannot be stopped.

(165)
10...Na5 traps the white queen.

(166)
21...Bh2+ 22.Kh1 Rxd5 takes advantage of the pinned e-pawn.

(167)
24...Rd1+ 25.Rxd1 Rxd1+ 26.Ke2 Qd2#.

(168)
24...Nh3#.

(169)
10...Nxd4#.

(170)
10.Nc7+ is a family fork.

(171)
23.Qa8+ leads to a back-rank mate, **23...Bc8 24.Qxc8+ Qf8 25.Qxf8#**.

(172)
48...Qf6#.

(173)
26.Qh8#.

(174)
11...Bb4 pins the white queen to the king.

(175)
34.Nd5 forks the black rook and bishop.

(176)
14...Qxc3 takes a piece that is attacked twice, and only defended once. On the previous move, White played **14.b3??** to prevent Nc4 forking the queen and rook, but allowed this instead.

(177)
25.Bxg7 Kxg7 26.Qf6+ forks the black king and bishop on c6. **26...Kg8 27.Qxc6** wins a piece.

(178)
58.Rxh6+ picks up a pawn, making the win even easier. **58...Kxh6** or **58...Kg7 59.Nxf5+** forks the black king and rook.

(179)
18.Bg6+ creates a discovered attack, **18...hxg6 19.Rxd7**.

(180)
10...Qc3+ forks the white king and rook.

(181)
43.Re8#.

(182)
38.Rg3 pins the black queen to the king.

(183)
32...g5 traps the white bishop. If **33.Kg4** attacking the black rook, **33...Be6** setting up a discovered check **34.Re7 Re5+** protecting the bishop with check.

(184)
21...Rxb5+ 22.Nxb5 Qb2#.

(185)
21...Qxh3!! and White cannot capture the queen with **22.gxh3** because of **22...Ne3+ 23.Bg6 Rxg6+ 24.Kh2 Rg2+ 25.Kh1 Rxh3#**.

(186)
18...Rb1#.

(187)
23...Bxc3 wins a piece, and removes the defender of the knight on b5, which is pinned to the king.

(188)
43.Rxh7 and White trades down into an easily won endgame.

(189)
37...b2 and the pawn cannot be stopped from queening.

(190)
17...Rh1+ 18.Ke2 Qxe1#.

(191)
19.Bxc5 wins a piece. Neither the black knight or black queen can recapture. **19...Nxc5 20.Qxf7+ Qxf7 21.Rd8#**, or **19...Qxc5 20.Qxf7+ Kh8 21.Qg8#**.

(192)
White wins a piece with **15.Qxf5!** If Black recaptures with **15...Qxf5 16. Nxg7+** picks up a pawn and forks the Black King and Queen.

(193)
30...Qxf3 and White cannot stop **31...Qxg2#**.

(194)
19...Re4 pins the white queen to the king.

(195)
31.Qb2+ and Black can only throw pieces in the way to delay mate, **31...Bc3 32.Qxc3+ Rd4 33.Qxd4+ Qe5 34.Qxe5#**.

(196)
19.a3 and the black knight has no good squares to go to. If **19...Nc6 20.Bxc6+** wins a piece, because of the threat **20...Qxc6 21.d5** with a double discovered attack on both the black queen and rook on h8 from the white bishop on b2.

(197)
25.Qf6 takes advantage of the pin on the black rook on f7 by the white bishop on d5, and threatens Qh8#. Black can only delay checkmate. For example, **25...Be5 26.Bxe5 Qxe5 27.Bxf7+ Rxf7 28.Rd8+ Rf8 29.Rxf8#**.

(198)
27...Ra2+ 28.Kc1 Bb2+ 29.Kc2 Ba3#.

(199)
28...g5#.

(200)
27.Bh7+ Kh8 28.Qf6#.

(201)
5...Nxf3+, and Black's queen is under attack, but he plays the check first to remove the defender. **6.Qxf3 Qxg5** wins a piece.

(202)
8...Na5 traps the white queen, who got greedy grabbing pawns.

(203)
42.Rd7# or **42.c7#**.

(204)
24.Rh3 and Black cannot stop mate, *24...Rfc8 25.Qh8+ Bxh8 26.Rxh8#.*

(205)
21...Rc1+ creates a discovered attack on the white queen, *22.Rxc1 Qxd4.*

(206)
17.Bxa7 Qa8 18.Nb6 traps the queen. This is also a good checkmate pattern to know.

(207)
16...f6 forks the white queen and bishop.

(208)
30.Rxf2!! ignores the fact that the white queen is hanging because of *30...Qxe4 31.Rf8#*, which is what happened in the game.

(209)
9.Bf7#.

(210)
5...Bxa3 removes the defender of the white bishop on c4. *6.bxa3 Nxc4* wins a piece.

(211)
20.Qc7+Ke6 or *20...Ke8 21.Qe7#.*

(212)
18.Bxh7+Kh8 19.Ng6# White sacrificed his queen to set up this pretty minor piece mate.

(213)
41.Nc6+ forks the black rook and king.

(214)
17.Rxf6 wins a pawn that appears to be defended, but isn't because the knight on d7 is pinned.

(215)
23...Bxf1, clearance. *24.Rxf1 Bxc3* wins a piece because of the pinned b-pawn, *25.bxc3 Rxb1.*

(216)
33.Rxb8+ simply takes the hanging rook with check. In the game, White was worried about the b-pawn, and played *33.Rxb4*. This is still winning, but clearly not as good. The game ended in a draw.

(217)
26.Rxc8 overloads the black defense. *26...Bxc8 27.d7* forks the black bishop and rook, *26...Rxc8 27.Rxe4.*

(218)
27.Rxf5 wins a piece. The g-pawn is pinned, and cannot recapture.

(219)
White is down a queen, but has powerfully placed bishops and a rook on a half open file that lead to mate with *24.Rxg7+ Kh8 25.Rxh7+ Kg8 26.Rh8#*. In the game, White missed the checkmate, and instead went for the windmill attack, *25.Rxf7 Kg8 26.Rxe7*, which is also winning.

(220)
15.Ne7+!! deflects the black queen, *15...Qxe7 16.Rh8+!!*. White got back to back double exclaims from Deep Rybka, *16... Kxh8 17.Qh3+ Qh4+ 18.Qxh4+ Kg8 19.Qh7#.*

(221)
18.Rxf6 takes advantage of the multiple pins. The g-pawn is pinned to the king, so cannot capture. *18...Qxg6 19.Rxg6*, or *18...Qxf6 19.Qxe8+* and White is up a piece either way.

(222)
8.Bxg7 wins an undefended pawn, and will win the rook as well.

(223)
16.Qd6+ Ke8 17.Rxg8#.

(224)
24.Qxh6 wins a piece. The black bishop on g7 is pinned.

(225)
16...Nb3+ forks the white king and queen.

(226)
7...Nd4+ 8.Kd1 Qxe1+ 9.Kxe1 Nxc2+ forks the white king and rook.

(227)
47.Rg7+!! creates a discovered attack, *47...Rxg7 48.Qxf5+.*

(228)
9...Qd4+ forks the white king and rook, ***10.e3 Qxa1***.

(229)
29...Bc3 cuts off all of the escape squares, and White cannot stop ***30...Ra1#***.

(230)
19.Bd4 pins the black queen to the king.

(231)
30...Bd4 pins the white rook to the king.

(232)
31.Ne5+ Ke8 32.Qd7# or ***31...Ke7 32.Ng6#***.

(233)
20.Bd5 skewers the black queen and f7-pawn, ***20...Qd7 21.Rxf7***.

(234)
23...Qa2 and White cannot stop ***24...Qa1#***.

(235)
14...h6 and the white queen has no good squares to go to. If ***15.Qg3 Nd3+*** discovered attack on the queen.

(236)
34...h5 attacks the trapped white rook.

(237)
31...Rc2 pins the white queen to the king.

(238)
40...g4#. White was up a queen for a rook, and on the previous move missed a one move tactic that would have forked the black king and rook. He grabbed the h7-pawn instead, and missed this mate in one.

(239)
40.Qb5+ forks the black king and rook. Instead of this crushing move, White played ***40.Qxh7***, winning a pawn, and was then mated with ***40...g4#.***

(240)
28...Rd2+. Black got the first move right, but missed the follow up mate in one, and went on to lose the game.

29.Kg1 Qxg2#
29.Ke1 Qe2#
29.Kf1 Qd1#

(241)
38.Ne7+ Kh7 or ***38...Kh8 39.Qxh5#***.

(242)
45.Qd7#.

(243)
32.c5+ creates a discovered check, winning the black queen, ***32...Qe6 33.Bxe6 Nxe6***.

(244)
26...Qh5+ 27.Kg1 Qh2#.

(245)
14.Bxf6 and Black cannot recapture because of the threat of ***Qxh7#***.

(246)
15.Qxh7#.

(247)
37.d4 forks the two black knights.

(248)
24.Rxg7+ Kxg7 25.Qe7+ checks the king, while adding a second attacker to the black rook on f8. ***25...Kh6 26.Rxf8*** and White has won a piece.

(249)
25.Be8 skewers the rook and knight. The rook cannot move and still protect the knight on g6.

(250)
35...Qh2#.

(251)
14.Nxd6+ forks king and bishop ***14...Ke7 15.Nxb7***.

(252)
43...Rg2+ 44.Be2 Bxe2#, Or ***43...Rh2+ 44.Kg1 Rg2#***.

(253)
29...Rxa1+ 30.Rc1 Rxc1+ 31.Qd1 Rxd1+ 32.Kh2 Qh4#.

(254)
31.Nxh6+ creates a double discovered check, ***31...***

Kh7 32.Nxf5 picks up the loose bishop, *31...Kh8* or *31...Kf8 32.Qg8#.*

(255)
23...Ne3+ forks the white king and queen.

(256)
24.Bxf7+ discovered attack *24...Kxf7 25.Rxd6.*

(257)
38.Rb8+ Kh7 39.Rh8#.

(258)
33...d4 attacks the white bishop on e3, and if the bishop moves, Black has Re2+ forking the white king and bishop on c2, winning a piece.

(259)
17.Bf4 and the black queen has no escape squares. Black will lose material.

(260)
22...Rce8 and the white queen has no escape squares.

(261)
33.Qe7 and Black cannot stop mate, *33...Qe5 34.Qxe5+ Kg8 35.Qg7#*
33...Qb7 34.Bg7+ Kg8 35.Qf8#
33...Qa7 34.Bg7+ Kg8 35.Qf8#.

(262)
23...Rxd5 takes the white knight while discovering an attack on the white rook on c8 from the bishop on e6. If *24.Rxd8 Rxd8* and Black is up a piece, If *24.exd5 Rxc8* (or *25...Bxc8*), and Black is up a piece in this variation as well.

(263)
61...c3 and the white bishop cannot stop both pawns. For example *62.Bb3 a2 63.Bxa2 c2* and Black will make a queen on the next move.

(264)
38...Re4!! forks the pinned white rook and bishop.

(265)
34...Nc3 forks the two white rooks.

(266)
30.Qxh7+!! Nxh7 31.Rxh7+! Kxh7 32.Rh3#.

(267)
15.b5 attacks the black knight, which has no safe squares to go to.

(268)
28.Rd8+ Rxd8 29.Rxd8#.

(269)
19.Bxb5+ discovered attack *19...Kf8 20.Rxc3.*

(270)
29...Qxe4. At first it appears that Black cannot take the hanging white queen because of the back-rank mate threat, but this isn't true. *30.Rd8+ Qe8 31.Rxe8+ Rxe8* and Black is up a rook.

(271)
35...Qe2+ 36.Kg1 Qe1+ 37.Rxe1 Rxe1#.

(272)
15.Na4 and the black queen has no safe squares to go to.

(273)
19.Bh3 attacks the black knight on d7, which is providing necessary defense of the black bishop on c5. Black cannot move the knight and still protect the bishop, and will lose material.

(274)
5...Bxb2 wins a pawn, and the white rook next.

(275)
18.Rf5 forks the black queen and reckless g5 pawn.

(276)
26.Qxg6, and the h7-pawn is pinned, *26...Qe7 27.fxe7 a6 28.exd8Q#*
26...Qe1+ 27.Rxe1 b6 28.Rxh7#
26...Rd7 27.Qe8+ Qf8 28.Qxf8#
26...Qxb2 27.Rxh7#.

(277)
9...Nxd3# smothered mate.

(278)
31...Rf8+ overloads the white king, *32.Kg3 Rxe1.*

(279)
30...Qf1+!! mate attack *31.Rxf1 Rxf1+ 32 Kg2. Rg1#,* Hook Mate.

(280)
32...Ra8 33.Qb4 Ra4 traps the white queen.

(281)
34...Bd4+ creates a discovered check. *35.Ke2 Re3+*, forks the white king and knight.

(282)
30...Rxg2+!! 31.Rxg2 Qxf3. 31.Qxg2 Qd1+ 32. Rf1 Qxc2 Black wins the white queen for a rook.

(283)
35.Rh5+ decoy: h5, *35...Kxh5 36.Qg5#.*

(284)
32.Rxa6 threatens Ra8# and leads to mate in 3, *32...bxa6 33.Qxa6+ Rb7* *(33...Kd7 34.Qb7# or 33...Kb8 34.Qa8#)* *34.Qa8+ Rb8 (34...Kd7 35.Qxb7#) 35.Qc6#.*

(285)
67...Nb6#.

(286)
26.Nc4 forks the black queen and rook.

(287)
52...Rh3 traps the white knight. If *53.Ng2 Rh2* pins the knight to the king, *54.Kb3 Rxg2.*

(288)
9...Bxg3+ takes advantage of the pinned h-pawn, *10.hxg3 Rxh1.* This is a common tactical idea in From's Gambit.

(289)
10...Qxd4#.

(290)
30.Qg4+ forces the black king to the h-file. After *30...Kh6 31.Rg8*, Black will not be able to prevent *Qh4#.*

(291)
20.Re1 pins the black queen to the black king.

(292)
11...Qb6 threatens both the White Bishop on b4 and checkmate on f2. White cannot meet both threats.

(293)
35.Nxe5+ forks the black king and bishop.

(294)
13...Rb8 skewers the white queen and bishop *14.Qd3 Rxb2.*

(295)
18.e7 forks the black rooks. *18...Bxb1 19.exd8=Q Rxd8 20.Rxb1* and White is ahead a knight for a pawn.

(296)
35.Qe8+ skewers the black king and queen, *35... Kf5 36.Qxe3.*

(297)
15.Ba4+ and Black has to give up the queen to get out of check.

(298)
25...Rxb4 wins a piece. The a3-pawn is pinned.

(299)
19.Nf6+ forks the black king and rook.

(300)
11...Bxc3+ wins a pawn. *12.bxc3 Qxc3+* forks the white king and rook *13.Kf1 Qxa1+.*

(301)
29...exf4 uncovers a pin on the white queen to the white king.

(302)
9.Nxe4 wins a piece that is just hanging. In the game White fell for Black's unsound trap and played 9.Bxd8??, which allows 9...Bxf2#.

(303)
9...Bxf2#.

(304)
14...Qd3+ 15.Bd2 Qxd2#.

(305)
15.Nc7#.

(306)
5...g6, and the white queen cannot move and still defend the knight on e5.

(307)
6.Bg5 attacks the trapped black queen. **6...Be7 7.Bxh6**, and Black cannot recapture because of the threat **8.Qxf7#**. If White played 6.Bxh6 right away, Black has the defense 6...Qf6 which defends the f7-pawn, and attacks both the white knight on e5 and bishop on h6.

(308)
7.Qxf7#.

(309)
16.Bg5 and the black queen has no good squares to go to. **16...Qe8 17.e7+** creates a discovered check, **17...Kh8 18.exf8=Q+**.

(310)
20.Rf8#.

(311)
14...Qxe5+ forks the white king and bishop.

(312)
19...Nh3#.

(313)
28...Qa3+ gets the black queen out of danger with check, not giving White enough time to save his queen, which is also under attack.

(314)
67.Ra4+ skewers the black king and queen.

(315)
17.Bh6 attacks the trapped black rook, which can't move.

(316)
27...Qd2#.

(317)
27.Rxe6 removes the defender of the rook on c8. If **27...Nc4+ 28.Rxc4 Rxc4 29.Rxe7**, and White has two minor pieces and a pawn for the rook.

If **27...Rxc1 28.Rxe7+**, in-between move check to save the White rook first. **28...Kf8 29.Kxc1** and White is up a piece.

(318)
19...Nb3+ forks the white king and rook. **20.Kd1 Rxe2** trades off the hanging rook first, **21.Kxe2 Nxa1**.

(319)
19...Qh4, and White doesn't have time to save the knight and avoid checkmate, so will lose a piece. For example, **20.f4 Qxh2+**.

(320)
18.d6 traps the bishop.

(321)
37...Rd1 skewers the white queen and knight, **38.Qc3 Qxd4+**.

(322)
28.b5 traps the black bishop.

(323)
18...Bf5 attacks the queen. If **19.Qf3**, then **19... e4** attacks the white queen and with a discovered attack on the bishop on b2.

(324)
9...Bg3+ discovered attack **10.hxg3 Qxd4**

(325)
32.Rxh7+!! a very nice sacrifice leading to checkmate. **32...Kxh7 33.Qh5+ Qh6 34.e5+** discovered check **f5 35.exf6+** en passant **Bf5 36.Bxf5+ Kh8 37.Qxh6#**.

(326)
28...Rxe3 29.fxe3 Bxe3+ forks the white king and rook. **30. Kf1 Bxc1**, and Black is up a piece.

(327)
38...Rxf4+! forks the white king and rook, trading down to a winning endgame. **39.Rxf4 Nxf4 40.Kxf4 e2**, and White cannot stop the e pawn from queening.

(328)
36...Qe6#.

(329)
14.Bxh7+ Mate attack **14...Kxh7 15.Rh3+ Qh4 16.Rxh4+ Kg8 17.Qh5 Nxe5 18.Qh8#. 14... Kh8** also leads to mate, **15.Rh3 Qg5 16.fxg5 g6 17.Bxg6+ Kg7 18.Rh7+ Kg8 19.Qh5 Nxe5 20.Rh8+ Kg7 21.Qh7#**. This is a good attack formation to know. The main components are the bishop check on h7, Black's lack of a knight on f6, the rook and queen's ability to swing to the h-file quickly, and the white knight on e5.

(330)
13...Nxf2 wins a pawn and forks the white queen and rook. If *14.Kxf2 Qf6+* forks the white king and rook on a1.

(331)
17...Qxd6 takes the white knight, getting Black out of check. It might appear that this falls for a trap with *18.Bb5+* but Black just plays *18...Ke7* and Black is up a piece.

(332)
33...Qb1, and the queen forks the rook and the bishop.

(333)
20.Qd4 threatens mate on g7 and attacks the b6-pawn. Black cannot meet both threats.

(334)
11...Re8 pins the white knight to the king, *12.Bf4 f6*.

(335)
10.Bd5 forks the black rook and knight.

(336)
21.Rxe6+ wins a piece. Black cannot recapture because of *21...fxe6 22.Bg6#*.

(337)
29.h3 forcing the rook to move. If *29...Rg6*, then *30.f5* forks the black rook and knight.

(338)
37...Be3 seals the fate of the pinned bishop on f2. *38.Rb2 Rxf2+ 39.Qxf2 Bxf2 40.Rxf2*, and Black makes a nice comeback gaining a queen for a rook.

(339)
13...e5 forks the white bishop and knight.

(340)
30...Qxf6!! wins the white rook. White can't recapture because of *31.exf6 Rxe1+ 32.Qf1 Rxf1#*.

(341)
53...Rxe6+, and Black trades down to a winning endgame, *54.Rxe6+ Bxe6 55.Kxe6 f3*.

(342)
12...Qb6 double attacks the white knight on a7 and the f2-pawn.

(343)
34.f6+ overloads the black king, *34...Kxf6 35.Rxd6*

(344)
41...Rf1+ skewers the white king and rook, *42.Kg3 Rxf6*.

(345)
23...Bg2+ 24.Kxg2 Ne3+ forks the white king and queen.

(346)
34...Bxb4, and White doesn't have time to recapture, because of *...Qh2#*.

(347)
42.Re8#.

(348)
49...Qh5+ 50.Kg1. Black mates with either *50...Qd1+ 51.Re1 Qxe1#* or *50...Qh2+ 51.Kf1 Qf2#*.

(349)
14.Ne7+ forks the black king and queen, and leads to a nice checkmate, *14...Kh8 15.Nxg6+ fxg6 16.Rh1+ Kg8 17.Rh8+ Kxh8 18.Qh1+ Kg8 19.Qh7#*.

(350)
29.Bb4+ discovered attack on the black queen, *29...Kc6 30.Rxa2*.

(351)
29...Rxf1+, and White can't recapture because of *30.Qxf1 Qh2#*.

(352)
12.Rxe5, and the knight on c6 can't recapture because it's pinned. White wins a piece.

(353)
9...Qb6 threatens both the hanging white bishop on b2 and *10...Qxf2+*. White cannot meet both threats.

(354)
17...Bf4 skewers the white rooks.

(355)
33...Rxh4+! 34.Kxh4 Qh5#.

(356)
20.Nhf5+ (or 20.Ngf5+) 20...gxf5 21.Nxf5+ forks the black king and queen, **21...Kh8 22.Nxe7.**

(357)
16.Qe4 forks the two black bishops.

(358)
10.e5 attacks the black knight on f6 and discovers an attack on the black pawn on c6 from the white queen. **10...Nd5 11.Nxd5 cxd5 12.Qxd5** and White wins a pawn.

(359)
11.Qxc6+ forks the black king, bishop on c5, and rook on a8.

(360)
14.Qe3+ forks the black king and rook on a7, **14... Ne5 15.Qxa7.**

(361)
18.Nf5, and Black cannot stop **19.Qxg7#.**

(362)
17...Bxg3 18.hxg3 Qxg3 wins a pawn.

(363)
27...Ne7 adds a second attacker to the white bishop on g6, which cannot be defended a second time. White cannot move the bishop because it is pinned to the white rook on f6. White will lose a piece.

(364)
8.Bf7+ leads to mate, **8...Ke7 9.Nd5+ Kd7 10.Qg4#** or **8...Kd7 9.Qg4+ Ke7 10.Nd5#.**

(365)
21.Nc7+ forks the queen and the king.

(366)
11...Nc3+, discovered check **12.Kf2 Nxd1+.**

(367)
23...Qe1+ 24.Kc2 [24.Kb2 Qxc3#] Qxc3+ 25.Kd1 Qd2#.

(368)
15. Qxa8! Qxa8 16.Nc7+ forks the black king and queen. **16...Kf7 17.Nxa8** wins a rook.

(369)
9.axb4 simply takes the black bishop. Black got a little too fancy with all the pins and potential knight forks.

(370)
27.Qe4+ Kh5 28.Qh7+ Kg4 29.Qf5#.

(371)
41...Qxd3+ forks the king and rook.

(372)
15.Nf7 forks the black queen and rook.

(373)
13...Bd4 wins a piece by attacking the unprotected white rook on a1, **14.Nc3 Bxc3 15.Rb1.**

(374)
24...Qh2#.

(375)
19...exd4, is a double attack on the white knight on c3, and a discovered attack on the white queen. Black wins a piece.

(376)
46.Qh3+ skewers the black king and queen. **46...f5 47.Qh6+**, and the black king cannot move and still guard the black queen, **47...Ke5 48.Rxd7.**

(377)
17.Rxh5!, and neither piece can recapture. The black queen cannot take because of **17...Qxh5 18.Qd8#**, and the black knight is pinned to the queen. White wins a piece.

(378)
33.Qh8#, and Black help mates himself on the previous move with **32...Qf7??.**

(379)
33...Bf4+34.Qxf4 Nh1+ 35.Kf3 Nh4#.

(380)
26.Bg6+ Kf8 27.Qh8#.

(381)
36...Ne1+ forks the white king and bishop. Black played the dubious Latvian Gambit opening in this game, and lost his queen in the opening, but did a nice job to come back and still win.

(382)
25.Nc7#.

(383)
33.Qd4 threatens mate on d7, the rook on h8, and the knight on b4.

(384)
38...Nxf3+ deflects the white queen. *39.Qxf3 Qxc5* forks the king and rook. If white plays *39.Kg2* then *39...Rh2+.40.Kxf3 Rxf2 41.Kxf2 Qxc5+*

(385)
40...Rh1+!! overloads the white king, if *41.Kxh1 Qxf2*, or if *41.Kg2 Rh2+ 42.Kxh2 Qxf2+.*

(386)
13...e4 attacks the white bishop on f3, and creates a discovered attack on the white rook on a1 from the black queen.

(387)
23.Bh7+ discovered attack *24...Kxh7 25.Qxh4.*

(388)
40...Rh8 pins the white queen to the king.

(389)
39.Qh8+ skewers the black king and rook, *39...Ke7 40.Qxb8.*

(390)
22.Nd4 forks the black rook and queen.

(391)
32.Rh1 saves the white rook, and threatens mate on the h-file.

(392)
42.Rg5#.

(393)
10...Nxf3+ removes a defender of the white bishop on g5 with check *11.Bxf3 Bxg5 12.Nxg5 Qxg5* and Black is up a piece.

(394)
17...Bxf3 removes a defender of the white bishop on d4, *18.gxf3 Bxd4.* If *18.Qxf3 Rxe1#*

(395)
15.Bxb8 trades off the Bishop with tempo, setting

up a tactic *15...Raxb8 16.Nd4* winning a piece. Black does not have time to move the Queen and protect the Knight on g4 which is now attacked twice, and defended only once.

(396)
33...Nc3+ forks the white king and rook.

(397)
12.Nd5 attacks the black queen and e7-pawn. Black cannot move the queen and maintain a defense of the black knight on d4, which is attacked twice, and defended twice. If *12...Qd8 13.Bxd4* wins a piece.

(398)
20.Nf6+ forks the black king and rook, *20...Kf8 21.Nxe8 Kxe8.*

(399)
24.Qf6, and Black can only delay checkmate with some spite checks. For example, *24...Qxg4+ 25.hxg4 Be4 26.Rxe4 Ne5 27.Rxe5 Kg8 28.Re8+ Rxe8 29.Qg7#.*

(400)
22.Rxf7+ discovered check, winning the queen, *22...Ke8 23.Rxf5.*

(401)
18.dxc6 attacks the black bishop on b7, pins the f7-pawn, and threatens mate. White wins a piece. If *18...Bxc6 19.Qxg6+ Kh8 20.Qg7#.*

(402)
6...Qa5+ forks the white king and loose bishop on g5, *7.Qd2 Qxg5.*

(403)
14.Qd5#.

(404)
31...Bd7 attacks the white queen, and unpins the black rook on f7. *32.Qh6 Rxf3* takes advantage of the pinned g-pawn.

(405)
54.Ne6+ forks the black king and rook.

(406)
10...Bxg5+ wins a piece. The knight is attacked twice and only defended once.

(407)
11.Qxh7#.

(408)
17...Bf4+ saves the bishop with a check. **18.Kb1 Bxd5**, and Black comes out ahead a piece.

(409)
25.Qxh7+ Kf8 26.Qh8#

(410)
22.Qg5+ Bg6 [**22...Kh7 23.Qg7#**] **23.Qxg6+**, (the f7-pawn is pinned) **23...Kh8 24.Qg7#** .

(411)
18.Bh6+ Kg8 19.g4 and the black bishop cannot retreat to g6 because of **20.Qxg6**. The f7-pawn is pinned.

(412)
28.Bc4 adds a second attacker and pins the black knight to the king. White wins a piece.

(413)
10.Nxc6+ double discovered check, forking the black king and queen.

(414)
36.Nxf6+ creates a discovered attack **36...Kf7 37.Rxd6 gxf6**. White wins the queen and pawn for a knight.

(415)
27...Rxc5 takes a piece that is attacked 3 times, and only defended twice. **28. Rxc5 Rxc5 29.dxc5 Qxc5** picks up a pawn.

(416)
14.Bb6+ discovered check, winning the black queen, **14...Kd8 15.Bxc7+**.

(417)
17.Nc6 forks the black queen and rook.

(418)
41.Nc8+ forks the black king and bishop, and allows the queen to protect the white rook on d1, which was under attack.

(419)
28.Nxf5! wins a pawn, attacks the black queen, and threatens Ne6+, forking the black king and rook. If

(420)
28...exf5 29.e6+ creates a discovered attack on the black queen from the white bishop on b2, **29...Kg6 30.Bxg7**.

(420)
22.Qf7+ Kh8 23.Qf8+ Rxf8 24.Rxf8#.

(421)
7.Qa4+ forks the black king and hanging bishop on g4, **7...Nc6 8.Qxg4**.

(422)
20...Nxb2 wins a pawn, attacks the white queen, and removes the defender of the white knight on c3, **21.Qb5 Bxc3**.

(423)
27...h6 attacks the defender **28.Rxa7 hxg5**.

(424)
34.R1b7+ Rc7 35.Rd8#.

(425)
23...Rfe8 traps the White Queen.

(426)
12.Bh3 pins the black queen to the king. This type of pin happens often when Black castles queenside.

(427)
20.b8Q+ makes a queen and the black knight on d7 is pinned to the king.

(428)
17...Bxd3 forking the white rook and queen.

(429)
18.Rxg7+ sets up a windmill tactic, **18...Kh8 19.Rxf7+ Kg8 20.Rg7+Kh8 21.Rxd7+ Kg8 22.Rg7+ Kh8 23.Rxb7+ Kg8 24.Rg7+ Kh8 25.Rxa7+ Kg8 26.Rxa8**.

(430)
24.Nxe4. In the actual game White moved his queen which is under attack, and missed this move which wins a piece. **24...Bxc5 25.Nf6+** forks the black king and queen. **25...Kg7 26. Nxd7** regains the queen, up a piece.

(431)
23.Rxe8+ forces the black king out into the danger zone, **23...Kxe8 24.Qe4+ Kd8 25.Qe7+ Kc8**

26.Qc7#. There are other similar mates, depending on how the black king moves.

(432)
28.Qh6 threatens **29.Qg7#**. Black's only way to stop the mate is **28...Qf8**, but this allows **29.Nxd5,** winning a piece, because of the weak back-rank. Black cannot recapture the knight. For example, **29...Qxh6 30.gxh6 Rxd5 31.Rxc8+ Rd8 32.Rxd8#**.

(433)
12.Ng5+, and Black is in big trouble. If **12... Kf8 13. Ne6+** forks the black king and queen.

If **12...Ke8 13.Bxg6+ hxg6 14.Qxg6+ Kf8 15.Ne6#** or **12...Kf6 13.Qc4 d5 14.Qxd5 cxb2 15.Qf7#**.

(434)
23...Rb1 pins the white queen to the king. Playing **23.Rfb8** first works as well.

(435)
23.Be5+ f6 24.Bxf6#.

(436)
28.Rc1 attacks the black bishop, which is pinned to the other bishop. Black cannot defend all these loose pieces. **28...Rb3 29.Bd2** adds a second attacker to the bishop. **29...Bxd2 30.Nxd2** forks the black rook and bishop, winning a piece.

(437)
38.Be4+ forks the black king and rook.

(438)
29.Ba3 pins the black knight to the king, and is the fastest win for White, **29...Kg8 30.Bxb4**.

(439)
32.b4 and the black knight on a5 has no good retreat squares. If **32...Nb7 33.Bxb7 Bxb7 34.Rxg4** wins a piece.

(440)
13.Rxc8+ Bxc8 14.Qc2 creates a double attack on the black bishop on c8 and black knight on a2.

(441)
18.Rh4 and Black cannot stop mate, **18...Re8 19.Qxh7+ Kf8 20.Qxf7#**.

(442)
19.Qg6#

(443)
51.b5# is a pure checkmate, each of the squares in the field of the checkmated king is controlled exactly once.

(444)
12.Qd8#.

(445)
15...Qxa1!, and White does not have time to recapture because of **16.Bxa1 d1=Q+ 17.Kb2 Rd2#**.

(446)
37...Rxf3+! wins a piece. If **38.Kxf3 Ne5+** forks the white king and rook.

(447)
52...Rd2#.

(448)
21...c6 attacks the pinned white knight on d5. **22.Nc7 Bxc4 23.Nxa8 Bxf1 24.Rxf1 Rxa8,** and Black comes out a piece ahead.

(449)
20.Qxd5! wins a pawn. **20...Qxd5 21.Nc7+** forks the black king and queen **21...Kd7 22.Nxd5**.

(450)
33.Qxh6+! is an X-ray attack, **33...Rxh6 34.Rxh6#**.

(451)
18...Rfd8 adds a second attacker to the white knight on d2, which cannot be defended a second time. Black wins a piece.

(452)
15...Bh2+ 16.Kh1 Bg3+ 17.Kg1 Qh2+ 18.Kf1 Qxf2#. This bishop and queen mating tango is a good one to know.

(453)
30.Qxh6+Kg8 31.Qh8#.

(454)
15...e4 forks the white bishop and knight.

(455)
9.Nb5, and Black cannot prevent **10.Nc7+** forking the black king and rook, **9...Rb8?? 10.Nc7+ Ke7 11.Bxc5#**.

(456)
20...Ne3 attacks the trapped white rook on d1.

(457)
45...Nf2+ forks the white king and rook.

(458)
27...Re4 forks the white knight and pawn on d4, which is now attacked twice.

(459)
10.c5 attacks the black queen, which cannot move, and still defend the rook on h2.

(460)
7...Bxe4 takes the knight, which is attacked twice, and only defended once. Black doesn't need to worry about the pin on his queen because **8.Qxe4 Nxe4 9.Bxd8 Kxd8** or **8.Bxf6 Qd5 9.Qf4 gxf6**, and Black is ahead a piece.

(461)
39...Nf2#.

(462)
18.Nc2 forks the black bishop and queen, adding a second attacker to the bishop.

(463)
5...g2+ discovered check. **6.Nxh4 gxh1=Q**, and Black is up a rook.

(464)
58...Ne3+ forks the white king and knight to clear the way for the pawn to promote, **59.Nxe3 a1=Q+**.

(465)
23...Bb4 traps the white queen.

(466)
Black would like to play **8...fxg3** but doesn't have time because of **9.Bf7#**, so needs to play something like **8...Nd5** or **8...Bg7** or anything that prevents the checkmate. In the game Black missed this threat, took the knight, and got checkmated.

(467)
26...Nc4+ forks the white king, bishop, and rook

(468)
36.Qa4#.

(469)
10.Ng5+ and Black has to give up the queen to avoid mate with **10.Qxg5 11.Bxg5**.

If **10...Kg8 11.Qe6+ Bf7 Qxf7#**.

(470)
21.Qc4 and Black cannot save both the bishop and pinned knight.

(471)
29...Nc3 forks the two white rooks.

(472)
22.Qxg6, and the h7-pawn is pinned.

(473)
24...Qxg2#.

(474)
24...Qh1+ 25.Ke2 Bf3+ 26.Kd2 Qxd1#.

(475)
30.e6+ overloads the Black king from the defense of the black rook on g8, **30...Kxe6 31.Rxg8**. If **30... Kf8 31.e7+ Kxe7 32.Rxg8**.

(476)
26.Nxg6+! wins a pawn, deflecting the black knight from the defense of c6, If **26...Nxg6 27.Rxc6**.

(477)
10.Re1 pins the black queen to the king.

(478)
12.Nxf6+ gxf6 (or **12...Rxf6**) **13.Rxd1**, not 12.Rxd1 Nxe4, which loses a piece. It is important for white to trade off the knights first, with check, before recapturing the queen.

(479)
43...Rb2 pins the white queen to the king.

(480)
20.g6 cuts off all escape squares for the black king. Black cannot prevent **21.Qh8#**.

(481)
27.Re7+Kd8 28.Rf8#.

(482)
12.e5 double attacks the black knight on f6 and rook on a8.

(483)
23.Qf7#.

(484)
22.Ne6 discovers an attack on the black queen from the bishop on g1, and threatens Qxg7#. Black cannot meet both threats.

(485)
7...e5 double attacks the white knight on c5 and the white bishop on f4.

(486)
40...Rdd2 adds a second attacker to the pinned white bishop.

(487)
24...Nxg3 overloads the f2-pawn defending the bishop on e3. If **25. fxg3 Rxe3** wins a pawn and bishop for the knight.

(488)
10.d4 attacks the black bishop and threatens the pawn fork **11.d5**.

(489)
55.Qa8+Qa5 56.Qxa5#.

(490)
13.Qe5+d6 [13...Bd6 14.Qxd6#] 14.Qxe7+ Nd7 15.Qxd6#.

(491)
41...Bc6+ skewers the white king and pawn on g2.

(492)
16.Qd8#.

(493)
28.Be5+ skewers the black king and rook.

(494)
14...d4 forks the white knight and bishop.

(495)
9.Qxf7#.

(496)
25.Qxf6 wins the knight. The g7-pawn is pinned.

(497)
9...Nd3# is a common trick in the Budapest Defense, which even experienced players fall for.

(498)
24...Bxd4 wins a piece. The bishop is pinned to the queen.

(499)
11.Re1 pins the black queen to the king. If **11...Be6** blocks the check **12. d5** forks the black bishop and knight.

(500)
20...c4 attacks the white bishop, which is the only piece keeping the h3 and c2-pawns safe from the black queen. White cannot move this piece, without losing some pawns. For example, **21.Be2 Qxh3**, and White's kingside starts to fall apart.

(501)
40...Ra1+!! deflects the hite king, so the pawn can queen, **41.Kb2 dxc1Q+ 42.Kxb3 Ra3+ 43.Kb4 Qc3#.**

If **41.Kxa1 dxc1=Q#**

(502)
23...Nxd4 wins a valuable central pawn. If **24.cxd4 Bxd4** forks the white king and rook.

(503)
18...Qxh3+ and since the g2-pawn is pinned, **19.Kg1 Qxg2#.**

(504)
15.Nd6+!! forks the black king and bishop on b7. If **15...Qxd6 16.Bb5+** creates a discovered attack.

(505)
22.Bd6+ Kc8 23.Qc4+ Qc7 [23...Qc6 24.Qxc6#] 24.Qxc7#.

(506)
21.Bd7+ forks the black king and queen.

(507)
8.Ne5 threatens Bxf7#, **8...Be6 9.Bxe6 fxe6 10.Qh5+ g6 11.Nxg6 hxg6 12.Qxh8**.

(508)
17.Qxf7#.

(509)
25...Qc7 forks the white knight and rook.

(510)
3...Qh4+ and White is already in big trouble, **4.g3 Qxe4+ 5.Qe2 Qxh1**. If **4.Ke2 Qxe4+ 5.Kf2 Bc5+**.

(511)
11...g6 attacks the white queen, which cannot move and maintain defense of the black bishop on e5.

(512)
48.Qf8#.

(513)
54.Rc8#.

(514)
16.Ra1 traps the black queen, **16...Qb2 17.Rfb1 Qxb1+ 18.Rxb1**.

(515)
7.e5 attacks the black knight, which is pinned to the queen.

(516)
33.Bxf5 wins a pawn. The e6-pawn is pinned.

(517)
52.Nd8+ forks the black king and pawn on c6, trading down to a winning endgame, **52...Ke8 53.Rxe7+ Kxe7 54.Nxc6+**.

(518)
36.Re8+ forks the black king and bishop, **36...Kh7 37.Rxc8**.

(519)
11...axb4 wins a pawn. The a3-pawn is pinned to the undefended rook on a1.

(520)
39.Be6# discovers checkmate, pinning the black queen.

(521)
12...Nxd2 wins a piece. White cannot recapture because of **13.Qxd2 Bb4** pinning the white queen to the king.

(522)
29...Rd1+ 30.Re1 Rxe1#

(523)
White had previously sacrificed his bishop on f7, thinking he would gain the piece back with 10.Ng5+ Kg8 11.Qxg4, but it doesn't work because of **10...Qxg5 11.Bxg5 Bxd1 12.Rxd1** and Black remains up a piece.

(524)
26.Rxf5+Ke8 27.Qxg8#.

(525)
22...d2 Black ignores the attack on his queen with the bigger threat of 23...d1=Q+. After **23.Bxd2 Qxe5**, Black is ahead the exchange.

(526)
9...Nxg4 simply takes an unprotected piece.

(527)
20.Bxh7+ creates a discovered attack on the black queen, **20...Kxh7 21.Qxd4**.

(528)
11.Qc4+ unpins the knight with check **11...Kh8 12.Nxe5**, winning a piece.

(529)
25.Re6+ leads to mate.

25...Be7 26.Rbxe7+ Kf8 27.Nd7#
25...Kd8 26.Rd7#.

(530)
31.Qxb7#.

(531)
38...Qxf4+ 39.Kh3 Nf2#.

(532)
30...Rd1+ 31.Ka2 Bd5+ forks the white king and knight, **32.b3 Bxe6**.

(533)
38...a3 and White cannot stop the pawn.

(534)
15.Nxh4 Bxh4 16.Qh5 is a double attack, threatening both Qxh7# and Qxh4.

(535)
22.Qg3+ Kf8 23.Qg7+ Ke8 24.Qh8+ Ng8 25.Qxg8# The queen and knight work well to deliver mate.

(536)
16...Ba6+ 17.Bb5 Bxb5#.

(537)
10...Qxf2+ takes a pawn, forking the white king and bishop, **11.Kd1 Qxg2.**

(538)
13...Qf2+ forces the white king to the d-file. **14.Kd1** sets up the pin **14...Rd8.**

(539)
22...Qxd4+ forks the white king and rook. Black started this combination with a knight sacrifice on d4 on the previous move.

(540)
27...Qxb1+ ! deflects the white bishop. **28.Bxb1 Rf1#** or **28.Qe1 Qxe1#.**

(541)
21...f4 and the white rook has no good escape squares.

(542)
40...f3 and the white rook cannot stop both pawns. For example, **41.Rg3 e2 42.Rxf3 e1=Q.**

(543)
7...Bxg2 takes a free pawn, and the rook the next move.

(544)
54...g6+ Overloads the white king **55.Kxg6 Qxg4+.**

(545)
11.Nxc7+ Ke7 12.Bc5#.

(546)
13.Bf6 and mate on g7 cannot be stopped, **13... Bxf2+ 14.Rxf2 Bxd3 15.Qg7#.**

(547)
15.Qf3+ Qf6 16.Qxf6+ Kg8 17.Qf7#.

(548)
16...Nxf2#.

(549)
11...e4 forks the white bishop and knight.

(550)
4...e5 is a decoy that forks the white bishop and knight. **5.Bxe5 Qa5+** forks the white king and bishop. **6.Qd2 Qxe5** wins a piece.

(551)
26...Rxd1+ gives Black's queen an escape square **27.Qxd1 Qd8.**

(552)
25...Nxc3 grabs a pawn with a discovered attack on the white queen and rook, **26.bxc3 Rxd1+.**

(553)
60...Rh2+ skewers the white king and knight. **61.Kf3 Rxb2.**

(554)
16...Bb5 skewers the white queen and rook.

(555)
15.e4 forks the black bishop and knight.

(556)
28.Qxh5#

(557)
37.Nxe6 takes a pawn and attacks the black queen. If **37...fxe6 38.Qxe6+** forks the black king and knight, **38...Kg7 39.Qxg4.**

(558)
38.Qe8+Bf8 39.Qxf8#.

(559)
20.Bg5 forks the two black rooks.

(560)
33...Ke3 and White cannot stop 34...Rh1+, which will either checkmate or skewer the white king and rook, if **34.Kf1 Rh1+ 35.Kg2 Rxc1.**

(561)
15...Rxd3! and White cannot recapture with the pawn because of **16.cxd3 Nb3+** forking the white king and queen.

(562)
34...Rh1#.

(563)
25.Nd5 attacks the black rook on e7 and creates a discovered attack on the black queen from the white queen. If **25...Qxe3** White has the in-between move **26.Nxe7+ Rxe7** and then recaptures the queen with **27.fxe3**, coming out ahead the exchange.

(564)
17.f5 traps the black bishop.

(565)
10...Rxd5 wins a piece since the e4-pawn is pinned.

(566)
25.Rxd6!!crashes into Black's camp, winning a pawn. The overloaded black queen cannot capture the rook and defend the mate threat of Qxf7# at the same time.

(567)
30.Ngf6+ forks the black king and rook. Choosing the knight on g4 is best, because after **30...Kh8 31.Nxd7** White is now forking the black queen, rook and bishop, which is now attacked twice.

(568)
26...Bc5 pins the white rook to the queen.

(569)
27.Nc6+ creates a discovered check **27...Kf8 28.Nxa5**, winning the rook.

(570)
44.Bg5 attacks the pinned bishop on e7, which cannot be defended a second time.

(571)
19...Rg8 attacks the white queen, which is pinned to the g2-pawn. White cannot move the queen because of **20...Qxg2#.**

(572)
31.Rf8+Rxf8 32.Rxf8#.

(573)
31...Rc8 attacks the white queen, which is pinned to the white rook, preventing a back-rank mate.

(574)
46...Rc2 and White cannot prevent **47...Rc1+** forking the white king and rook and promoting to a queen, **48.Rxc1 bxc1=Q+.**

(575)
32.Nxe6 takes the hanging queen. In the game White played 32.Nxd7 instead, which removes the defender of the rook on b8, which is not as good.

(576)
25.Qc6#

(577)
13.Bxd5 wins a piece and pins the black queen to the king.

(578)
19...Qxf2#.

(579)
8.Re1 pins and wins the black queen.

(580)
19.Bc7#.

(581)
12.Qe6+ Kf8 13.0-0-0+ (or 13.Rf1+) **Qf6 14.Rxf6+ gxf6 15.Bh6#.**

(582)
34.Rd7# is a nice checkmate with the rook and bishop working well together.

(583)
7.Bg5 traps the black queen. This pattern happens a lot in games between lower rated players who tend to develop their queens too early. The black knight would be better placed on f6.

(584)
7.Qh5# is a fools mate pattern.

(585)
14.Bxb7 grabs the undefended pawn, and White will take the rook on a8 on the next move.

(586)
16.Bf4 attacks the black queen with tempo. After the queen moves, White will be able to play **17.Nxc7+**, forking the black king and rook.

(587)
7...Qxg5. Nothing fancy, just taking a hanging piece.

(588)
29...Qxg4!! 30.hxg4 Ng3+ forking the king and queen. Black wins a rook.

(589)
6...Qxb2 grabs a pawn, and Black will also win the rook on a1.

(590)
60...Rxe3+ 61.Kg8 Re8#

60...Re6+, 60...Re4+, 60...Re5+ and *60...Rd7+* also lead to checkmate in a similar manner.

(591)
44.Rf1 pins the black bishop to the king, *44...h6 45.Rxf3+.*

(592)
46...Rxd3+ and *47.Kxd3 Bc4+* skewers the white king and rook.

(593)
8...Nc2+ forks the white king and queen.

(594)
13...Re8 pins the white bishop to the king, and saves the pinned black queen, *14.Kf1 Rxe6.*

(595)
10.dxc3 captures the black bishop with the pawn, so the white queen protects the white bishop on d5.

(596)
17.Rd8#.

(597)
32.Qh6+ Kg8 33.Qg7#.

(598)
21...Qxd4+ captures the bishop, forking the white king and rook.

(599)
26.Bd5+ interferes with the black queen's protection of the rook, *26...Rxd5 27.cxd5.*

(600)
40.g4 traps the black bishop.

(601)
20...Rxe5 takes advantage of the pinned d4-pawn to win a piece. If *21.Rxe5 Qxe5.*

(602)
25...Qh2+ 26.Kf1 Qh1#.

(603)
9.Qxh7# is a very common mating pattern with queen and bishop.

(604)
21...Rxb3 creates a discovered attack on the white rook on a5 from the black bishop on c3. White doesn't have time to capture the black rook and protect his own rook. Black wins a piece.

(605)
12...Qf6 forks the white rook on a1 and the vulnerable f2-pawn.

(606)
31.Rf1+ Kg5 32.Nf7+ forks the black king and rook, *32...Kh4 33.Nxd6.* White wins the exchange.

(607)
47.Rf7#.

(608)
27...Qxc4+ forks the white king and rook.

(609)
10.dxc5 attacks the black queen and removes a defender of the knight on b4. After the black queen moves, White can play *11.Bxb4.*

(610)
12.Qh5+ g6 13.Nxg6 hxg6 14Qxh8 and White is ahead a rook and pawn for the knight. *12...Ke7 13.Bb4+*, and Black is in big trouble.

(611)
29...Qh1#.

(612)
19.Bc3 skewers the black queen and g7-pawn, *19...Qd5 20.Bxg7.*

(613)
48.Rb1 pins the black queen to the king, *48...Qxb1+ 49.Qxb1+.*

(614)
16...exf4, White has two piece hanging – the bishop on f4 and knight on f8. Taking the bishop first is best, because the knight has no good escape squares. *17.Nxh7 Kxh7* and Black is up a piece.

(615)
27.Bd5+ and Black will have to use the queen to block the check.

(616)
17...Qg4 18.Kh1 Qxg2#.

(617)
52.Ra4+ deflects the black king from the defense of the black rook. If *52...Kf3 53.Ra3+ Kf4 54.Rxg3.*

(618)
34.Rd8+ chases the king away, so the pawn can queen, *34...Ke7 35.c8=Q Rxc8 36.Rxc8.*

(619)
34...Rd1+ 35.Bxd1 Rxd1+ 36.Kg2 Rd2+! overloads the white rook. *37.Kf3 Rxc2* X-Ray wins a piece, *38.Qxc7 Rxc7.*

(620)
37...Nxe4 takes a pawn that is attacked twice, and defended once. Black doesn't have to worry about the pin *38.Re2* because of *38...Nxf2 39.Rxe6 fxe6 40.Kxf2.*

(621)
20.Rh8+ Kxh8 21.Bxg7+ discovered attack *21...Kxg7 22.Qxd6.*

(622)
26...Ne2+ wins the queen. The bishop is pinned.

(623)
22...Bxf2+ wins a pawn, and sets up a knight fork. *23.Kxf1 Ne3+* forks the king and queen, *23.Kh1 Bg2+ 24.Kxg2 Ne3+..*

(624)
21...Rab8 gets the rook out of danger, and skewers the white bishop and b2-pawn, *22.Bxa6 Rxb2.*

(625)
18.Bxc3, and Black cannot recapture because *18...Qxc3 19.Bxb5+* creates a discovered attack *19...Kf8 20.Rxc3.*

(626)
30.Qc3+ f6 31.Qxf6+ Rg7 32.Qxg7#.

(627)
17...Bf5 skewers the white queen and rook *18.Qd2 Bxb1.*

(628)
24.Nxc5 Bxb1 25.Rxb1 and White has two bishops for the rook, which is a good trade.

(629)
29.Bf5 traps the black rook, *29...Rxf3 30.Nxf3.*

(630)
25.Qe4 attacks the black knight on d5 and threatens checkmate with Qh7# *25...Qc5+ 26.Ne3 Rfb8 27.Qxd5* and White is up a piece.

(631)
10.Qxf7#.

(632)
11...Nc2#.

(633)
20...Bxc3 removes the defender of the knight on d2, *21.bxc3 Rxd2.*

(634)
12...Qxe3+ takes a pawn that is attacked twice, and only defended once.

(635)
13...Bxc4 wins a piece. The white queen is overloaded defending the white knight on b1.

(636)
8...Na5 traps the white queen.

(637)
7.exd5, and Black has two pieces attacked by pawns, and cannot save both.

(638)
42...Qxh2+!! 43.Kxh2 f3+ discovered check *44.Kh3 Rh1#.*

(639)
11.Qd8#.

(640)
13.Rh3 and Black cannot prevent mate.

(641)
44...Qc2+ skewers the white king and queen, **45. Ke1 Qxg2**, if **45.Kf1 Qd1#**.

(642)
23...Bh3+ 24.Rxh3 Qxh3#.

(643)
21.c5 traps the black bishop.

(644)
15.Bg6#.

(645)
25...Be4 The bishop pins the rook on f3.

(646)
7.d4, the pawn forks the black knight and bishop.

(647)
27...e5 attacks the pinned white knight, and will win it on the next move, **28...exd4**.

(648)
20...Qc4 threatens both the loose rook on f1 and the knight on b3 (the c2-pawn is pinned), **21.Rf2 Qxb3**.

(649)
20...Qb6+ forks the white king, knight and bishop, which is now attacked a second time, **21.Bc5 Qxb5**.

(650)
23...Rxc2 takes a piece that is attacked twice and only defended once.

(651)
31.Qxe6, and both queens are under attack, so White takes out the black rook first. Black doesn't have time to recapture and save his own queen, **31...Qxg2+ 32.Kxg2 fxe6**.

(652)
40.Rf5+ Kh6 41.Qg5#.

(653)
20.f6 threatens **21.Qxg7#** if **20...g6 21.Qh6**, and mate cannot be stopped.

(654)
38...Re2#, and the tiger catches its prey.

(655)
16...Qe1#.

(656)
41.c6 creates a mating net with the threats of **c7#** and **Rd7#**, which Black cannot stop.

(657)
24.Qf4+ forks the black king and rook on h6. Then **24...Bd6 25.Qxh6**.

(658)
28.Rxe6 the pawn can't recapture because it is pinned by the rook.

(659)
43...Rg2#.

(660)
24.Bg5+ creates a discovered attack on the black rook. **24...Qxg5 25.Qxe4** (or **25.Rxe4**) wins the exchange.

(661)
10...Nxf4, and if White recaptures then **11.Nxf4 Bb4** pins the white queen to the king.

(662)
32...Bxd4+ takes a pawn that is hanging, and forks the white king and knight.

(663)
19.Bxf6 takes a piece that is attacked twice and defended once.

(664)
26.Be4 skewers the black queen and rook.

(665)
32.Rxf8+ Kxf8 33.Re8# or **33.Qe8#**.

(666)
White has mate in two with either **34.Ne4+ dxe4 35.Qc5#** or **34.Nb7+ Bxb7 35.Qc7#** (or **35.Qc5#**).

(667)
29.Re8#.

(668)

32...Nh3+!! clearance. *33.Rxh3*, or *33.Qxh3 Qxf2+34.Kh1 Qxe1#*, or double attack *33.gxh3 Qxf2+ 34.Kh1 Qxe1+*. If *33.Kh1* Black has a beautiful smothered mate with *33...Nxf2+ 34. Kg1 34.Nh3+ 35. Kh1 Qg1+ 36. Rxg1 Nf2#*

(669)

39.Bxf6+ Re7 40.Bxe7#.

(670)

28.Qh6 and mate cannot be stopped, *28...Rxe1 29.Qg7#*.

(671)

31...Rxc1 trades off the hanging rook first. *32.Rxc1 Nf3+* forks the white king and queen (the g2-pawn is pinned), *33.Kf2 Nxh4*.
Extra Credit: White can get the queen back with *34.Rc8+ Kf7 35.Rc7+*, which skewers the king and queen. After *35...Kg8 36.Rxg7+ Kxg7* Black is still up a knight.

(672)

23.Nd6+ forks the black king and queen.

(673)

16...Bxh4 17.gxh4 Qxh4 wins a pawn.

(674)

24.Rxa8 sets up a fork that wins a piece, *24...Nxa8 25. Qxd7 Qxd7 26. Nf6+*
In the game White played *24...Rxd7*, which sets up a similar fork, with *24...Nxd7 25.Qxd7. 25...Qxd7 26.Nf6+* forks the black king and queen, and White is up a knight after *26...Kg7 27.Nxd7*.
Taking the rook with 28. Rxa8 is better, because White comes out ahead a rook instead of a knight, but both variations win a piece.

(675)

14...Nc6 attacks the white bishop on d4 and discovers an attack on the white queen from the black rook on f8.

(676)

40.Qb7#.

(677)

36.Rc7 adds a second attack to the f7-pawn, which cannot be defended a second time. All of Black's pieces are tangled up on the queenside.

(678)

26.Bh7+ Kh8 27.Bg6+ Kg8 28.Qh7+ Kf8 29.Qxf7#.

(679)

16.Qxd4 wins a piece. The black knight on f5 is pinned.

(680)

17...Bxd4+. Black has two pieces under attack and he can't save both so he first trades the bishop for a pawn with check. Now after *18.cxd4 Qxb5* Black is up a pawn.

(681)

25.Qd4+, and Black has no good way to get out of check. If *25...Rf6* or *25...Qf6* then *26.Nxf6*. If *25...Kg8* then *26.Qg7#*.

(682)

17...Rde6 adds a second attacker to the bishop on e2. If *18.Kf1* to defend it a second time, *18...Bxg2+* wins a pawn, since *19.Kxg2 Rxe2*.

(683)

29...h6 deflects the white queen from the defense of the white knight on b5, *30.Qd2 Qxb5*.

(684)

29.Bd5+ creates a discovered attack on the black queen, *29...Kh8 30.Qxe3*.

(685)

19.Qg4+ double attacks the black king and knight on e4, *19...Kf7 20.Bxe4*.

(686)

11.Ne6+!! clearance, *11...Kg8 [11...Bxe6 12.Qxd8#] 12.Qxd8+ Bf8 13.Qxf8#*.

(687)

34.f4 forks the black knight and rook.

(688)

17.Rd8+ Rxd8 18.Rxd8#.

(689)

23...Nxe3 wins a pawn, and removes the defender of the white knight on d4. The black knight cannot be captured.

If *24.Qxe3 Rxb1+ 25.Qe1 Rxe1+ 26.Rxe1 Bxd4*.
If *24.fxe3 Qxg2#*. After *24.Nf3 Nc2* forks the white queen and rook.

(690)
42...Bd5+ forks the white king and rook.

(691)
18.Bxg4, Black just left his bishop hanging, so White takes it.

(692)
8.Bxf7+ Ke7 9.Nf5#.

(693)
24...Rxc1+ 25.Rxc1 Rxc1#.

(694)
17...Nxf2 forks the rook and queen.

(695)
42...Qf3+ forks the white king and rook, *43.Kg1 Qxd1+*, which leads to a forced mate, *44.Kg2 Re2+ 45.Kf3 Qd3+ 46.Kf4 Qe3+ 47.Kf5 Qxg5#* or if *43.Rf2 Qh1#.*

(696)
25...Rxg3 wins a valuable pawn. The h-pawn is pinned.

(697)
28.Qg3+ and Black has to give up material with *28...Rd6* or *28...Qd6* or get smother mated. *28... Ka8 29.Nc7+ Kb8 30.Na6+ Ka8 31.Qb8+ Rxb8 32.Nc7#.*
If *28...Kc8 29.Nxa7#* or *29.Qc7#.*

(698)
20...Nd3+ forks the white king, rook, and bishop.

(699)
19.Qxe6+ takes a pawn with check, and adds a second attacker to the black bishop on d6, *19...Kh7 20.Bxd6.*

(700)
24.Rg3+ Kh5 25.Qh3#, and *24...Kh6 25.Qxg6#* or *24...Kh4* or *24...Kf4 25.Qg4#.*

(701)
18...Nxa3 takes a pawn, and forks the black queen and rook.

(702)
23.Nc5 with the idea of *24.Nb7* and *25.Nxd8* and Black cannot move the rook or else White will

queen the pawn. One sample line is *23...b6 24.Nb7 Bf6 25.Nxd8 Bxd8*, and White is up the exchange with a dangerous pawn on the seventh rank.

(703)
11.Qh5+ Ke7 (or *11...Kf8*) *12.Qf7#*

(704)
43...Re7+ creates a discovered check, winning the exchange, *44.Rxa7 Rxa7.*

(705)
15.Rdf1 threatens the trapped queen. Black will lose material. One option is to sacrifice the knight to save the queen. *15...Nc5* attacks the white queen, *16.dxc5 Qxc5.*

(706)
34.Qg4+ Ng5 35.Qxg5+ Kh7 36.Qg7#

(707)
26.Rxe5 wins a pawn and protects the white knight on g5. Black cannot capture the rook because of *26...Rxe5 27.Qxh7+ Kf8 28.Qf7#.*

(708)
44.Rb6+ pushes the king from the defense of the c6-pawn, *44...Kc8* or *44...Ka8 45.Rxc6.*

(709)
18...Bxh2+! wins a pawn, as the white knight on f3 is pinned to the white queen on e2.

(710)
21...Ba6 pins the white queen to the white king.

(711)
32...Nh3+ 33.Kh2 [*33.Kf1 Qxf2#*] *Qxf2+ 34.Ng2 Qxg2#.*

(712)
14.Rd4 forks the black bishop and queen.

(713)
28.Qf8+ Rxf8 29.gxf8=Q#.

(714)
16.b4 and the black queen has no safe squares that maintain protection of the black bishop on e5. Black's best option is to give up the black bishop for a pawn with *16...Bxh2+ 17.Kxh2 Qh5+.*

(715)
32...Rh1+ 33.Kg2 [33.Qg1 Rxg1#] Rg1+ 34.Kh2 Rh8+ 35.Qh3 Rxh3+.

(716)
14.Bxh6 Bxh6 15.Qh5+Kd7 16.Qxh6 wins a piece.

(717)
17.Bf3 skewers the two black rooks.

(718)
38.Rxb3 takes the passed black b-pawn with a discovered attack on the black rook on a6. Black cannot move the rook and maintain protection of the black bishop on b6.

(719)
38...Qe5+ forks the white king and rook.

(720)
47...g5+ 48.Kf5 Qf6#.

(721)
26.Qh6+ forks the black king and rook.

(722)
35...Rg1+ and White will have to block with the queen to get out of check, *36.Qd1 Rxd1+.*

(723)
33.Ra7 attacks the black bishop, which has no good escape squares. If *33...Bb4 34.Nd5* forks the black rook and bishop.

(724)
37...Qf4+ 38.g3 Qxf2+ 39.Kh1 Ra1#.
If *38.Kg1* or *38.Kh1 Ra1#.*

(725)
15.Re3 and Black cannot stop *16. Rh3#* without giving up major material.

(726)
21.Nb6 attacks the black queen and bishop, *21...Qc6* (or *21...Qd8*) gets out of the way. *22.Bxf6* removes a defender of the black bishop, *22...exf6 23.Nxd7 Qxd7 24.Bxb5* captures a pawn and skewers the black queen and rook.

(727)
35...Rd3#.

(728)
13.Be4 attacks the black rook on a8, which cannot be defended.

(729)
19.Nf6+ forks the black king and queen.

(730)
52.a7, and the white pawn cannot be stopped.

(731)
18.Rxg7+!! is a sacrifice that ends the game, *18... Nxg7 19.Nf6+* forking the black king and queen. If *18...Kh8 19.Rxf7+* wins the black queen with a discovered check.

(732)
24.Qh6#.

(733)
17...Qxh2+ 18.Kf1 Qh1+ 19.Ke2 Qxg2+ 20.Kd3 Ne5#.

(734)
44.Nxg5 is an unpleasant surprise for Black, winning a pawn. Black cannot recapture because of *44...hxg5 45.h6*, and the pawn cannot be stopped.

(735)
24...Qxh2+!! 25.Rxh2 Rxh2 26.Bh6 White can only delay mate *R8xh6 27.Qh3 R6xh3 28.Rxd4 Rh1#*

(736)
12.Nxf7! forks the black queen and rook, winning a vulnerable pawn. The knight cannot be captured. If *12...Kxf7 13. Qe6+* leads to a forced mate. *13...Kg6 14.Qf7+ Kf5 15.g4+ Kxg4 16.Qxg7+ Kh4 17.Qg5+ Kh3 18.Qg3#* or *13...Kf8 14.Qf7#* or *13...Ke8 14.Qf7#.*

(737)
40...Bb5 pins the white rook to the king.

(738)
25...Nxc3 wins a pawn with a double discovered attack on the white queen and rook. If *26. bxc6 Rxd1+ 27.Rxd1 Rxd1+* and Black is up the exchange.

(739)
11...Nxd4 wins a pawn with a discovered attack on the white queen. *12.Qxd7* and Black has the

in-between move *12...Nxe2+ 13.Kh2 Rxd7*, and Black is up a piece.

(740)
23...Rh1+!! deflects the white king from defense of the queen, *24.Kxh1 Qxf1+*.

(741)
8...Qc5 forks the white bishop and knight.

(742)
30.Nf2 double attacks the black bishop and rook. If *30...Rxd2* White has the in-between move *31.Nxe4+ Kf5 32.Nxd2*. White is up a piece.

(743)
15.Rxe5 wins a piece. The d6-pawn is pinned to the black queen.

(744)
39.Qxb8+! and White takes home the point. *Qxb8 40.Ra8* pins the black queen to the king, *40...Qf8 41.Rxf8+ Kxf8 42.b8=Q+*.

(745)
19.Re4, and the black queen has no good escape squares, *19...Qh5 20.Rh4*.

(746)
15.exd5+ creates a discovered check, attacking the black knight on c6. *15...Ne7 16.Bc7* traps the black queen.

(747)
46...Qd5 double attacks the g2 pawn threatening mate, and adds a second attacker to the white bishop on a5. White cannot defend both.

(748)
24...Qxf3 Black's queen is under attack, and Black's rook is attacking White's queen. By playing Qxf3 Black's queen goes into desperado mode, and White doesn't have time to recapture the black queen and save his own queen, so Black gains a piece.

(749)
16...b4 and the white knight on c3 cannot move because of the mate threat *17...Qxc2#*.

(750)
22.Nb5 attacks the black queen on c7 and pawn on d6. Black cannot defend both, *22...Qa5 23.Nxd6*.

(751)
26.Rd7# is a hook mate.

(752)
14...Nxc2 clears the way for the d-pawn to queen. *15. Nxc2 d1=Q 16.Rxd1 Rxd1* and Black gains a rook for the pawn.

(753)
11.Nc7+ family fork

(754)
19...e4 forks the white queen and knight, *20.Qe3* pinning the e4-pawn to the black bishop on e7, *20...f4 21.Qe1 Rxb3*

(755)
9...Nxd4 simply takes a piece that isn't protected, *10.Bxd7 Nxd7*.

(756)
15...Rxe3 removes the defender of the white knight on d4. *16. Rxe3 Bxd4* pins the rook to the king and attacks the rook on a1. *17.c3 Bxe3+ 18.Qxe3*, and Black comes out ahead a whole bishop.

(757)
7...Nxf3+ Black first trades off the knight that was attacked, with check. *8.Qxf3 Bxb5* coming out ahead a piece. The move order is important here. Playing *7..Bxb5 8.fxe5 Bxf1 9.Qxf1* is also good for Black, coming out ahead the exchange, but being ahead a whole piece is better.

(758)
22...Qxf3+ 23.Qxf3 Bxf3#.

(759)
18...Nxg5 takes a piece that is attacked twice and only defended once.

(760)
12...Nxe2+ deflects the queen. *13.Qxe2 Qxg5* wins a piece.

(761)
12...Nb4 attacks the weak c2-pawn, which cannot be defended. *13. Kf1* prevents the knight fork of king and rook *13...Nxc2*.

(762)
25...Be3+ forks the white king and knight.

(763)
10...d4 attacks the pinned bishop on e3, **11.0-0 dxe3**.

(764)
16...Qd5+ 17.Be4 Qxe4+ 18.Qf3 Qxf3#.

(765)
15...Nf3+ forks the white king and queen.

(766)
13...Qxf2+ overloads the white queen, **14.Kh1 Qxc2** if **14.Qxf2 Rxd1#**.

(767)
23...Bf4, and the white rook will get overloaded if White tries to hold on to everything. For example, **24.Rd3 Bxd2 25.Rxd2 Rxc3**. White's best chance is just to give up the exchange, and allow **24...Bxe3**.

(768)
23...Qxd1#. Black missed this mate in one in the game, playing Bg4 instead to skewer the rooks, and went on to lose the game.

(769)
26...Qc3#. This mate in one was missed in the game, with Black playing Qxa4+ instead, but this mating pattern was found by Black 2 moves later.

(770)
33.Bh6+ Ke7 34.f8=Q#.

(771)
27...Rc1+ 28.Ne1 Rxe1# with a back-rank mate. In the game, Black played 27...h6, worried about White's back-rank mate threat of 28.Nc6+ Ne8 29.Rxe8#, and missed his own back-rank mate.

(772)
48...Nf4+ forks the white king and rook.

(773)
18...Qxc2#.

(774)
7...Qa5+ forks the king and white bishop on c5.

(775)
57...Bc6+ forks the white king and knight.

(776)
42.Ne8+ Kf8 (or **42...Kg8** or **42...Kh7**) **43.Nf6+ Kg7 44.Rg8#**.

(777)
19.Rxf6 wins a pawn. The bishop on e5 is pinned.

(778)
19.Qxe5 takes the knight, which is attacked twice and only defended once.

(779)
22...exf5 wins a pawn. The e4-pawn is pinned to the rook on h1.

(780)
32...Ne3+ 33.Kg3 [33.Kh3 Rf3#] h4+ 34.Kh3 Rf3#.

(781)
18.Bxa7+ creates a discovered attack. **18...Kxa7 19.Rxe5** picks up a pawn.

(782)
19.Nd4 attacks the queen, which gets overloaded trying to defend the black knight on g4 and black bishop on e7. For example **19...Qd7 20.Bxe7 Qxe7 21.Qxg4** wins a piece.

(783)
22.Rxc6 removes the defender of the e7-square. Black doesn't have time to recapture because of **22...Bxc6 23.Ne7+** forking the black king and queen.

(784)
25...Nc5 forks the white rook and bishop.

(785)
19...Qxf3+ wins a rook. The e2-pawn is pinned, if **20. exf3 Rxe1+**.

(786)
13.d5 forks the black bishop and knight.

(787)
42.d7, and Black cannot stop the pawn from queening.

(788)
32.Ba4 traps the black rook, which has no good escape squares.

(789)
17.Ng5+ forks the black queen and king.

(790)
13.d5 forks the black bishop and knight.

(791)
42.f6 attacks the black rook and creates a passed pawn. If **42...exf6 43.e7** and Black has no good way to prevent the pawn from queening.

(792)
17.Qh8#.

(793)
29.Bh7+ overloads the black king. **29...Kxh7 30.Rxf8** wins the exchange.

(794)
19...Be5 skewers the white queen and rook.

(795)
25.Rde1 skewers the black queen and knight. **25...Qc6 26. Rxe5** wins a piece.

(796)
22...Bd6+ 23.Ke6 Qc4#.

(797)
15.Bf4 attacks the black queen, which cannot move and still defend the black bishop on e7, which is attacked from the white knight on f5.

(798)
15.e4! creates a discovered attack on the black queen and black bishop on f5. The black queen cannot move and still defend the black bishop on b4, **15...Qd7 16.Qxb4**.

(799)
17.Bb5 pins the black queen to the king.

(800)
36...Qxf2+ 37.Kh1 Qxg2#.

(801)
32...Rc1+ forks the white king and queen.

(802)
18...Bxd2 and a discovered attack wins a piece.

(803)
27...Re1#.

(804)
29...Qb1+ 30.Rc1 Qxc1+ 31.Qe1 Qxe1+ 32.Nf1 Qxf1+ 33.Kh2 Rxf2# (**33...Qg2#**)
or **32...Rxf2 33.Kh1 Qxf1#**
or **32...Qxf2+ 33.Kh1 Qg2#**.

(805)
37...Qf3+ 38.Kg1 Qg2#.

(806)
24...Rb1+ 25.Rd1 Rxd1#.

(807)
25...Qf3 and mate on g2 cannot be stopped, **26.Qxf7+ Rxf7 27.hxg5 Qxg2#**.

(808)
7.Nxh7+ removes the defender **7...Rxh7 8.Qg6#**.

(809)
10...Bb4!! pins the white queen to the white king. If **11.Qxb4 Nc2+** is a family fork.

(810)
10.Nd5#.

(811)
20.f5 attacks the black knight, which has no good escape squares. If **20...Nc7 21.Qc3+** forks the black king and knight on c7, attacking it for a second time.

(812)
28...Rxg3+ wins a piece. The f-pawn is pinned by the black bishop on c5.

(813)
20...Nf2#.

(814)
28...Bxf2+ deflection **29.Rxf2 d1=Q+. 29.Kh2** (or **29.Kh1**) **Rh8+ 30.Rh4 Rxh4#**.

(815)
37.Rb2 and Black cannot stop Rh2# **37...Rxa2 38.Rxa2 Kxh4 39.Rh2#**.

(816)
25.Qf8#.

(817)
16...g5 traps the white knight, which has no escape squares.

(818)
22.Nf4+ forks the black king and queen.

(819)
16.Qxh6#. This move was actually missed in the game, and White played **16.Rg6** instead.

(820)
7...Bc2 8.Qe1 Nd3 traps the white queen.

(821)
18...Rxf3 removes the defender of the d4-pawn, **19.gxf3 Nxd4**. Black is attacking the white bishop on b5 and has multiple knight forks that will win a second pawn, and the exchange back with either **Nxf3+** or **Nxb3+**. Black comes out 2 pawns ahead.

(822)
24.Qf7+ Kg5 25.h4+ Kxh4 26.Qf4#.

(823)
22.Nxb6+ forks the black king and queen. The c7-pawn is pinned by the white rook on c1.

(824)
29...Qh1#.

(825)
31...Re1 and the d2-pawn will become a queen.

(826)
24...Rxg3+ Removing the guard with check. If **25. fxg3 Qxe4**

(827)
28.Qxd6+! Kxd6 29.Bb4+ creates a discovered attack on the black queen. **29...Kc6 30.Rxa2** and White gains a piece.

(828)
5...Bd6 threatens mate with **...Bg3#**. White must push the d or e-pawn to create luft. **6.d4 Bg3+ 7.Kd2 Nf2** forks the white queen and rook, and White's position is a mess.

(829)
20.Nxf7 forks the black queen and rook.

(830)
21.Qf8# is a good mating pattern to know.

(831)
21...Bc5!! pins and overloads the white queen, **22.Qxc5 Rxg2+ 23.Kh1 Qh3#**.

(832)
22. c4 If the knight retreats to c7, this takes away the only escape square for the queen after **23.c5**.

(833)
40...Rf2+ 41.Kd1 or **41.Ke1 Qh1#**. If **41.Kd3 Qd4#**

(834)
28.h4 pins and wins the black bishop, **28...h6 29.hxg5**.

(835)
19.Bxc5 wins a pawn and attacks the black queen. **19...Nxc5 20.Qxe7 19...Qxc5+ 20.Qxc5 Nxc5 21.Rxe7**. White ends up ahead a pawn and rook for a knight.

(836)
23...Nc2+!! forks the white king and queen, and leads to mate **24.Kf1 Nxe3+ 25.Kg1 Qxf2+ 26.Kh2 Qxg2#**. The knight cannot be captured because of **24.Rxc2 Rd1#**

(837)
17.Ra5 traps the black queen.

(838)
54.Qg5+ forks the black king and rook.

(839)
33.Bxc5 and the black bishop on f8 is pinned and cannot be defended a second time.

(840)
48.Bf8+ and White can celebrate victory, **48...Kxf8 49.Qxf6**.

(841)
24.Bc7 attacks and traps the black rook that is preventing the pawn from promoting.

(842)
23.Ra1 traps the black queen. Black's best defense is **23...Nxc3 24.Rxa2 Nxa2**.

(843)
15...Nxe4 wins a pawn with a discovered attack on the white queen from the black bishop on g7.

(844)
22.Bc5 creates a discovered attack, pinning the black queen to the king.

(845)
33.Qxc5#.

(846)
9.Re1 pins the black queen to the king.

(847)
10.Bxh7 simply takes the hanging rook.

(848)
5...Nxf3+ removes the defender of the bishop on g5 with check. **6.Qxf3 Qxg5** wins a piece.

(849)
9.f7#.

(850)
28.Nxf6+ forks the black king and rook. The e7-pawn is pinned.

(851)
29...Rh1#.

(852)
32.Qg7+ Kxh5 33.Qxh7+ Kg4 34.Qh3#.

(853)
7.Nxe5 takes the knight, threatening **8.Bxf7# 7...e6 8.Qxg4** and White is up 2 pieces.

(854)
12...Qa5 forks the white knight and bishop.

(855)
30.Qg7+ Ke8 31.Qg8+ Kd7 32.Qxf7+ Kd8 33.Qe7#.

(856)
32.h4 kicks the knight, weakening the defense of the f7-pawn and e4-pawn. **32...Ne6 33.Bxe4+** or **33.Rxf7+.**

(857)
23...Nxf3+ removes the defender of the white bishop on h4, **24.Rxf3 Qxh4.**

(858)
29...Nf4 threatens the white queen, and threatens the smothered mate **30...Ne2#.** The game continued, **30.Qf3 Ne2+** and White had to give up the queen, **31.Qxe2 Rxe2.**

(859)
32.Nxf6+ forks the black king and both rooks. The g7-pawn is pinned.

(860)
9.Bxd5 and White wins a piece, because the e6-pawn is pinned. If **9...exd5?? 10.Qxc8+.**

(861)
16.Qxg5. White's queen is pinned to the king, but he turns lemons into lemonade with this move. **16...hxg5 17.Rxh8+** skewers the black king and rook. **17...Ke7 18.Rxa8,** and White has 2 rooks and a bishop for the queen. **18.Nd5+ Ke6 19.Bg4+,** skewering the black king and queen is also very good.

(862)
27.Qxf5 wins a pawn. The e6-pawn is pinned.

(863)
28...Rxd1+. Black sacrificed his queen on the previous move to set up this checkmate, **29.Kh2 Rh1#.**

(864)
16...Bb4 skewers the black queen and rook.

(865)
28...Bc8 attacks the rook on a6, and discovers the threat of **29...Re1#.** White cannot meet both threats.

(866)
18...Ra8 19.Qxb7 Rfb8 traps the white queen.

(867)
30...Rc8 attacks the overloaded white knight on c3, which is preventing the back-rank mate and defending the white bishop on d5. White cannot protect everything, for example, **31.Bxe6 Rxc3 32.g3** protects against the back-rank mate. Then **32...fxe6,** winning a piece.

(868)
13...Bxh3 takes a pawn, and threatens **14...Qxg2#.** The g2-pawn is pinned.

(869)
22.Rxc4 wins a piece. If **22...Qxc4 23. Nd6+** forks the black king and queen.

(870)
29.Bh7+ Kh8 30.Ng6#.

(871)
23.Nxg7+ forks the black king and queen.

(872)
19...Nxg4 and if **20.Qxg4 Nf6 21.Qh3** is the only safe square for the queen. **21...g4** forks the white queen and rook.

(873)
17.Ng5 threatens **18.Nxe6** forking the black queen and rook and mate with **18.Qxh7#**. Black cannot meet both threats.

(874)
24.c3+ Kc5 25.b4#.

(875)
49.Qe8#.

(876)
17.Bxb5 wins a pawn as the a6-pawn is pinned. If **17...axb5 18.Rxa8.**

(877)
10.dxe5 dxe5 11.Nxe5 wins a pawn.

(878)
12.Nxf7 wins a second pawn, and forks the black queen and rook.

(879)
14.dxc5 forks the black bishop and rook. If **14...Bxc5 15.Na4 Bd6 16.Nxb6** wins the exchange.

(880)
22.Qh8#.

(881)
26...Bb7 threatens the white queen and mate next move with **27...Qg2#.** White cannot meet both threats.

(882)
15.Bg5+ creates a double discovered check, **15... Ke8 16.Bb5+ c6 17.Bxc6+ Bd7 18.Bxd7#.**

(883)
37...Rc5#.

(884)
20...Bxh3 wins a pawn, and attacks the pinned white bishop. **21.Kh2 Bxg2** wins a piece.

(885)
31.Rd8+ Kc7 32.Bb6#.

(886)
13.Bxg5 forks the black queen and rook.

(887)
22...Qe2+ 23.Kc1 Qxc2#.

(888)
52.Rf7#.

(889)
21.Qc3+ forks the king and rook. **21...Kb8 22.Qxb4**

(890)
16.Nd7 forks the two black rooks.

(891)
12.Bh7+ creates a discovered attack on the Black queen with check and wins it in exchange for a bishop. **12...Kxh7 13.Qxd4.**

(892)
22...Rae8 pins and wins the white bishop.

(893)
23...Qb6+ and White can only throw pieces in the way to delay the inevitable, **24.Rd4 Qxd4+ 25.Kh1 Qa1+ 26.Qd1 Qxd1+ 27.Re1 Qxe1#.**

(894)
26...Bc5+ 27.Kg2 Rg1#.

(895)
29.Qg4+ Qg6 30.Qxg6+ Kh8 31.Qg7#.

(896)
22...Qxf4+ 23.Kh1 Qf3+ 24.Kh2 Bd6#.

(897)
14...Rxd1#.

(898)
36...h6#.

(899)
45...Kf5 uses the king as an offensive weapon to cut off key squares, **46.e8=Q Rd3#.**

(900)
16.Nxd7+ Nxd7 17.Qh8# or **16.Qh8+ Ke7 17.Nc6#.**

(901)
39.Rxf6. The e7-pawn is pinned.

(902)
39.Rd4#.

(903)
9...e5 forks the white bishop and knight.

(904)
17...Ne4 forks the white queen and bishop, which is attacked for a second time. **18.Qh2 Qxd6** (or **18...Nxd6**) wins a piece.

(905)
22...Rxg2+!! creates a discovered attack, **23.Kh1 24.Qxh4.**

(906)
5...Bb4 pins the white queen to the king.

(907)
16...Bxh2+ creates a discovered attack on the white queen, **17.Nxh2 Qxd5.**

(908)
11...Qf4#.

(909)
27...Qg2#.

(910)
33...Rxf1+ 34.Kxf1 Qe2+ forks the white king and bishop, **35.Kg1 Qxd2.**

(911)
12...Ne2+ forks the white king and queen.

(912)
11.Bxe4 takes a piece that is just sitting there undefended. Nothing tricky.

(913)
17.Nf7+ forks the black king and queen.

(914)
20...Rd3 forks the white knight and g3-pawn. If **21.Ne2** to defend the pawn **21...Rxe4.**

(915)
8.Ne6+ forks the black king and queen.

(916)
31...Ra1+ leads to a back-rank mate. **32.Re1 Rexe1#** or **32...Raxe1#.**

(917)
18.Rxd6+ is a mating attack, taking advantage of the pinned c7-pawn. **18...Ke7 19.Nd5+ Kf8 20.Qxc8+ Qd8 21.Rxd8#** or **18...Ke8 19.Qxc8+ Ke7 20.Nd5#.**

(918)
20.Na7+ deflects the king away from the rook with check. **20...Kb8 21.Rxd8#** is the end of the story for black.

(919)
18.Nxe4 takes the pawn (the d5-pawn is pinned). If **18...dxe4 19.Qxd7.**

(920)
8.Qd5 threatens the rook on a8 and the pawn on f7 (which will be captured with check and black will lose the bishop on f8). Black cannot defend against both threats.

(921)
16.d5 discovered attack on the black rook on h8. **16...Qxd5 17.Bxh8.**

(922)
14.Nxd5! If **14...cxd5 15.Bxd5+** forks the black king and rook.

(923)
23.e7 forks the black queen and knight. If **23...Kxe7 24.Bc5+** creates a double discovered check, skewering the black king and queen.

(924)
25...Bxd4. If **26.Rxd4** the knight forks the king and rook with **26...Ne2+.**

(925)
12...Bh2+ creates a discovered attack, **13.Kxh2 Qxd4.**

(926)
32...Rb1#.

(927)
15.Nxe5. If the pawn recaptures **15...dxe5**, then **16.Bg6#.**

(928)
21.Bxf6+! and all roads lead to mate:
21...Kh7 22.Qg5 Qxb2+ 23.Rxb2 b5 24.Qg7#
21...Kf8 22.Qh6+ Kg8 23.Qh8# (or **23.Qg7#**)
21...Kg8 22.Qg5+ Kh7 23.Qg7#
21...Kxf6 22.Qg5#

(929)
30...Bf2 forks the white rook and pawn on g3.

(930)
18.Rh8+!! 18...Kxh8 19.Qh2+ Qh4 20.Qxh4+ Kg8 21.Qh7#.

(931)
28.Qxf5!! wins a piece because of the pinned e6-pawn and back-rank mate threat of Rxe8#. For example, **28...Qxf5 29.Rxf5 exf5 30.Rxe8#.**

(932)
25.Ne4 adds a fourth attacker to the pinned bishop on c5. Black cannot defend it a fourth time, and if the bishop moves, **25...Bxd4 26.Rxc8.**

(933)
28.Bxb6+ removes the defender. **28...Kxb6 29.Rxd7** wins a piece.

(934)
6.d4 Bb6 7.d5 attacks the pinned black knight on c6.

(935)
24.Rxe6 and Black cannot recapture because of **24...Rxe6 25.Qf8#.**

(936)
13.Bxf6 Qxf6 or **13...gxf6 14.Nd5** forks the black queen and bishop.

(937)
47.Rd8#.

(938)
9.Nxc7 forks the black queen and rook.

(939)
16...Qc4+ creates a discovered attack on the white queen from the black rook, **17.Kf2 Rxe3.**

(940)
24...Bh6+ removes the white king from defense of the white bishop on d1, **25.Kb2 Rxd1.**

(941)
6.Qh5#.

(942)
8.Ne6 traps the black queen. Colorado chess player Paul Grimm calls this a "queen mate."

(943)
12...Qb6 wins a pawn. Black threatens the b4 pawn and a nasty discovered check. **13.bxc5 Qxc5+** forks the white king and bishop. **14.Rf2 Qxc4** and Black gets back his piece, ahead a pawn.

(944)
16...Qxe2 wins a piece. If **17.Qxe2 Ng3+** forks the white king and queen.

(945)
42...e2 and White cannot stop the pawn from queening.

(946)
48.Nxf6+Kh8 [**48...Kf8 49.Qe8#**] **49.Qe8+** [or **49.Qh5+ Qh7 50.Qxh7#**] **49...Qg8 50.Qxg8#.** White needs to be careful not to trade queens, because of insufficient mating material.

(947)
36.Qb8+ forks the black king and rook and leads to mate **36...Rc8 37.Qxc8+ Kf7 38.Qe8#.**

(948)
21...Rxf3 removes the defender of the white queen. **22.Qxh5 Rxf1+ 23.Rxf1 gxh5** and Black is up a knight.

(949)
18.Nxb6 forks the black rook and queen.

(950)
40...Qf3+ 41.Ke1 Qe3+ 42.Kd1 [**42.Be2 Qd2#**] **42...Qd2#.**

(951)
25.f4 attacks the black queen and black knight on h5, **25...Qf6 26.Bxh5**.

(952)
39...Qg2+ 40.Ke1 Bd2#.

(953)
19.Qxh6. The g7-pawn is pinned.

(954)
33...Qxf3! wins the rook. The g2-pawn is pinned.

(955)
7.Nd5 adds a third attacker to the pinned knight on f6, which cannot be defended a third time. Black will lose a piece.

(956)
11.Qxh7#.

(957)
10.Bxh5 creates a discovered attack, pinning the black queen to the king.

(958)
32.Bd8 attacks the pawn chain at its base. Black cannot protect the backwards b6-pawn.

(959)
34...Qxf3 wins the white rook, and threatens mate on the next move. The g2-pawn is pinned.

(960)
25...Qe1+ 26.Bf1 f2+ 27.Kh1 Qxf1#.

(961)
10...Bg4 pins the white queen to the king.

(962)
15...Bb5 skewers the white queen and rook.

(963)
21...Qxc1+ 22.Rxc1 Rxc1#.

(964)
28...Nb3 forks the white queen and rook.

(965)
10.Qa4+ forks the black king and knight on a6, **10...Qd7 11.Qxa6**.

(966)
33...Qh1#.

(967)
9...dxe4 attacks the white knight on f3 and creates a discovered attack on the white queen. White cannot save both. If **10.Qxb7 Na5** traps the queen.

(968)
11.Nxf6#

(969)
38...Ng2+ forks the white king and rook.

(970)
18...Nd4 attacks the white queen and bishop, adding a second and third attacker to the bishop – one by discovered attack. Black wins a piece. This is a good tactical idea to know, and is easy to miss.

(971)
8.e5 forks the black knight and bishop.

(972)
14...Qf3#.

(973)
16...cxb2+ creates a discovered check, winning the white rook on a1.

(974)
31.Ne6#.

(975)
39...Rf3 pins the white queen to the white king.

(976)
16...Be2 attacks the trapped white rook.

(977)
30.Qh6 and Black cannot stop **Qg7#**.

(978)
18.Ne6 forks the queen and rook.

(979)
14.Qxe5 and the knight on c6 can't recapture because it's pinned. White wins a piece.

(980)
13...Bxc3+ removes the knight from guarding the pawn on d5. **14.bxc3 Nf6** attacks the white queen.

15.Qa4 Qxd5 and Black wins back a pawn, and saves the trapped black bishop on e6.

(981)
21...Rxe3+ 22.fxe3 Qxe3+ 23.Qe2 Qxg1 and Black is up two pawns.

(982)
18...Qc3+ forks the white king and undefended rook on a1.

(983)
15...d4 forks the bishop and knight.

(984)
17.Qb4+ Kg8 18.Ne7+ Kf8 19.Ng6+ creates a double discovered check **19...Kg8 20.Qf8#**.

(985)
14.Qh4+ Nf6 15.Qxf6#.

(986)
28.Bxf4 wins the pawn. The g5-pawn is pinned and cannot recapture.

(987)
39...Nh3+ forks the white king and queen.

(988)
13...c4 forks the bishop and knight.

(989)
35.Rxf5 wins the rook. If Black recaptures **35...gxf5 36. Bf6#**

(990)
17...Bxd4+ takes a pawn that appears to be protected by really isn't, because it removes and deflects the defenders of the White Knight on e5. **18.Nxd4 Qxe5**

(991)
8.e5 forks the bishop and knight.

(992)
17...Rc8 pins the queen to the king winning the queen for a rook.

(993)
12...Qxd2#.

(994)
13...Qe4 and the queen threatens the white rook on b1 and a dangerous check on e1. All roads lead to heavy material losses for White.

(995)
6...Qh4+ 7.Kd1 Nf2+ creates a family fork and **8.Ke1 Nxd3+** creates a double discovered check, **9.Kd1 Qe1#**.

(996)
24...Rc3+. 25.Re3 blocks the check, then **25... Qxc1**, or **25.Ne3** blocks the check, then **25... Rxe3+! 26.Rxe3 Qxc1**.

(997)
18.Qf7#.

(998)
16.Rh8+!! Kxh8 17.Qh7#

(999)
5.Qa4+ forks the black king and knight. White set a trap with the opening moves, 1.e4 c5 2.Nf3 d6 3.c3 Nf6 4.Be2 leaving the e-pawn hanging, hoping for 4...Nxe4?? which allows this trap.

(1000)
26.Bxb7+ Qxb7 27.Qxb7#

(1001)
19.g4 forks the black queen and bishop.

Final Thoughts

Questions Or Comments?

We would love to hear your thoughts. If any of the problems were confusing we would be happy to help explain the answer. Email Tim at tim@tacticstime.com and Anthea at nth_carson@yahoo.com.

Other Books by Tim and Anthea

If you enjoyed this book, be sure to check out the first book in the series, *Tactics Time! 1001 Chess Tactics from the Games of Everyday Players*.

We also have a Kindle book for children and players just learning the game, *399 Super Easy Chess Tactics*, that features very simple tactics, such as one move captures: www.amazon.com/Super-Easy-Chess-Tactics-ebook/dp/B00AAQCBGU.

Acknowledgements

We could not have done a project like this without all of the people who take the time to enter their games into the computer, post their games on the internet, and have sent me their game collections to use. These include:

Paul Anderson	Bob Crume	William Parker
Pete Short	Robert Rountree	Aravind Suresh
Francisco Baltier	Carl Hamre	Priyav Chandna
Fred Spell	Ed Stoddard	Randy Reynolds
Jerry Maier	William Parker	Tim Tran
Bill Chandler	Eric King	Aaron Pauls
Shannon Fox	Geoff Chandler	Allan Ong
Dean Brown	Rob Hartelt	Gunnar Andersen
Chris Peterson	Jeff Baffo	Katie Wise
Brian Wall	Johnny Mac	Rhett Langseth
Richard 'Buck' Buchanan	Kenzie Moore	Isaac Martinez
Joel Johnson	Edson Cortiano	Daniel Gompf
Andy Pineda	Tomasz Pintel	Jason Chamberlain

Many other people sent us games as well, and we are very thankful!
Entering games by hand from score sheets into a PGN format can be a painful job, and we are fortunate that there are a lot of people who spent hours doing this.
Thank you to readers who helped us edit and catch errors, and provided good ideas and feedback, including:

Joey Guitian	Hank Anzis	Elizabeth Kestler
Peter Horecky	Dan Heisman	Deborah Natelson
Fred Jarmuz	Graham Diggins	Brendan Dolan
Art Cunningham	Andy Smith	Brian Wall
Joel Johnson	William Parker	Richard DuMerer
Geoff Chandler	Tijs Van Oevelen	Gil Baron
Stephen Dann	Barak Yedidia	Ben Franklin
Chris Kim	Joel Lecorre	Paras Gudka
Edson Cortiano	Richard Sloanaker	Bill Haynes
Jon Wooldridge	Ivan Busulwa	Daniel Winkler
José de Anchieta	Tim Paterson	Ken Wyatt
Jeff Davis	Josh Bloomer	René Pijlman
Rodolfo Pardi	Gunnar Andersen	Nigel Colter

Bill Haynes and Brian Wall were especially helpful, providing extremely detailed and invaluable feedback. Thank you!

We are also grateful to the following websites that helped to provide us with games:

www.coloradochess.com
www.renochess.org
www.redhotpawn.com
www.nwchess.com
www.metrowestchess.org
games.groups.yahoo.com/group/
UnorthodoxChessOpenings/
wyomingchess.com/
www.taom.com/pipermail/brianwall-chesslist/
cschess.webs.com/
eagleandking.webs.com/
www.angelfire.com/co/cscc/
www.chessclub.com
www.timmybx.com
www.denverchess.com
columbiachess.com/

kansaschess.org
georgiachess.org
www.scchess.org/
www.pscfchess.org
www.sdchess.org/
www.lincolnchessfoundation.org
nsca.nechess.com/
www.burlingamechessclub.com
www.westmichiganchess.com
ficsgames.com/
www.reddit.com/r/chess/
www.chess.com
www.idahochessassociation.org/
www.wachusettchess.org/
http://www.boylstonchessclub.org/

Don't Forget

To get more fun chess tactics from real player games, along with tips and tricks to help improve your chess game, subscribe to the award winning **Tactics Time Chess Improvement E-Mail Newsletter** at tacticstime.com/newsletter. It's free!

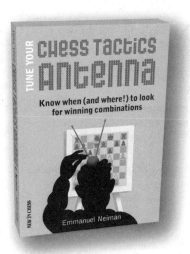
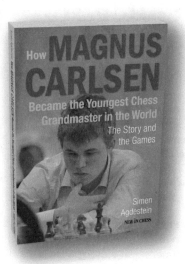

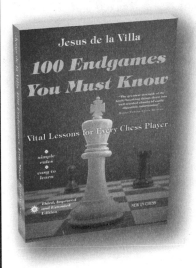